CW01652536

Ford
Escort

All UK models, Sept 1980 to 1982

(Does not cover Van models)

Owner's Handbook/Servicing Guide

by Peter G Strasman

ABCDE
FGHIJ
KLM

Haynes
THE BOOK

(806-11M1)

Acknowledgements

Thanks are due to the Ford Motor Company for the supply of technical information and certain illustrations. Valuable advice on lubrication was given by Castrol Limited, and on spark plugs by the Champion Sparking Plug Company. Special thanks must go to all the people at Sparkford who helped in the production of this Handbook.

A book in the Haynes Owner's Handbook/Servicing Guide Series.

Published and printed by the Haynes Publishing Group, Sparkford, Yeovil, Somerset BA22 7JJ

ISBN 0 85696 806 4

Contents

Ford Escort three-door Hatchback Saloon

Ford Escort five-door Hatchback Saloon

What's in it for You?

Whether you've bought this book yourself or had it given to you, the idea was probably the same in either case – to help you get the best out of your Ford Escort, and perhaps to make your motoring a bit less of a drain on your hard-earned cash at the same time.

Garage labour charges can easily be several times your own hourly rate of pay, and usually form the main part of any servicing bill; we'll help you avoid them by carrying out the routine services yourself. Even if you *don't* want to do the regular service and prefer to leave it to your Ford dealer, there are some things you should check regularly just to make sure that your car's not a danger to you or to anyone else on the road; we tell you what they are.

If you're about to start doing your own servicing (whether to cut costs or to be sure that it's done properly) we think you'll find the procedures described give an easy-to-follow introduction to what can be a very satisfying way of spending a few hours of your spare time.

We've included some tips that should save you some money when buying replacement parts and even when you're driving; there's a chapter on cleaning and renovating your car, and another on fitting accessories.

Apart from the things that every owner needs to know to deal with mishaps like a puncture or a blown light bulb, we've put together some Troubleshooter Charts to cover the more likely of the problems that can crop up with even the most carefully maintained car sooner or later.

There's also a set of conversion tables and a comprehensive alphabetical index to help you find your way round the book.

If the bug gets you, and you're keen to tackle some of the more advanced repair jobs on your car, then you'll need our Owner's Workshop Manual for your particular model. These manuals give a step-by-step guide to all the repair and overhaul tasks, with plenty of illustrations to make things even clearer.

Ford Escort XR3

Ford Escort Estate Car

The Escort Family

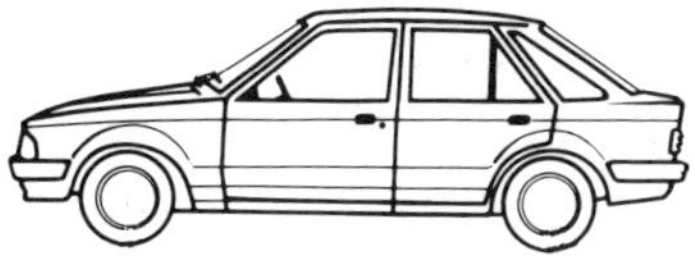

The 'new' Escort breaks tradition with the previous Escort models in that it is a front wheel drive vehicle powered by a transverse configuration engine.

The range was initially released in September 1980 in Hatchback form only, with Estate versions and a high-performance XR3 version following in November of that year. The Hatchback is available in either three- or five-door versions, the Estate and XR3 models being available in only three-door form. Depending on engine size, there are three basic levels of trim; L, GL and Ghia, as well as, of course, the sporting XR3.

Perhaps two of the most interesting features of the Escort range are the newly developed 'CVH' overhead camshaft used in most models, and the distinctive 'bustle-back' body styling for the Hatchback.

The CVH (Compound Valve angle, Hemispherical combustion chamber) engine has a five main bearing iron cylinder block with a light alloy cylinder head. The design of the cylinder head (from which the 'CVH' designation is derived) is such that the engine provides good fuel economy and power for its capacity, coupled with the low emission levels associated with efficient burning of the fuel mixture. Valve operation is via hydraulic tappets, which provide quiet operation with the added benefit that periodic adjustment is not necessary. The engine is mounted transversely and drives the car through a four- or five-speed gearbox, the five-speed becoming available on certain models from February 1982. The latter gearbox offers, of course, the added advantages of improved fuel economy and lower engine speed for a given road speed. This makes high-speed cruising much more relaxed with the accompanying reduction in engine noise.

The unusual 'bustle-back' styling of the Hatchback versions provides the car with a certain amount of individuality amongst so many other hatchbacks on the market today. It also helps to add to the efficient aerodynamic shape which achieves an exceptionally low drag coefficient.

The remaining mechanical components of the vehicle are fairly conventional, suspension being provided by MacPherson struts at the front, with wishbones and coil springs at the rear. Steering is by rack and pinion, and braking is provided by the normal front disc/rear drum arrangement. Generally speaking, most systems are designed with low maintenance requirements in mind. The electronic ignition system (not applicable to 1.1 models), clutch, brakes, wheel bearings etc are all routine maintenance free, requiring attention only when renewal of certain items becomes necessary.

As is the normal Ford custom, a wide range of optional extras and accessories is available to complement the basic trim levels.

With the wide availability of genuine and pattern spare parts, these vehicles are ideal for the home mechanic who wishes to keep running costs to a minimum.

Road Test Data taken from Autocar

The figures published here are extracts from *Autocar* magazine road tests.

Fuel consumption: The mpg figure is the overall consumption figure for their test period, including performance testing. Many owners will achieve significantly better consumption figures. The formula on the right provides a guide ('**mpg**' refers to the quoted overall test figure).

Driving style	*Driving conditions* severe	average	easy
Hard	-10%	**mpg**	+10%
Average	**mpg**	+10%	+20%
Gentle	+10%	+20%	+30%

	1.1 Hatchback 4-speed	**1.3 Hatchback 4-speed**	**1.6 Estate 4-speed**	**1.6 Hatchback 5-speed**	**XR3 4-speed**
Maximum speed (mph)	92	96	103	101	113
Overall fuel consumption (mpg)	36.9	31.8	32.1	32.1	27.9
Fuel consumption (mpg) at constant:					
30 mph	N/A	N/A	56.1	48.6	58.7
50 mph	N/A	N/A	43.9	43.9	45.7
70 mph	N/A	N/A	33.2	32.8	34.8
Range on full fuel tank (miles)	325	280	282	282	245
Acceleration (seconds):					
0–30 mph	4.4	3.7	4.0	3.7	3.5
0–40 mph	6.8	5.8	6.2	5.6	5.1
0–50 mph	10.6	8.3	8.4	8.0	6.9
0–60 mph	15.5	12.5	11.9	11.1	9.2
0–70 mph	22.7	17.5	16.7	16.3	13.0
Standing start $\frac{1}{4}$ mile	20.2	18.9	18.7	18.6	17
40–60 mph in normal top gear	15.4	12.6	11.0	16.9	7.4

The data given is for a typical cross-section of the Escort range only – figures for your particular car may vary.

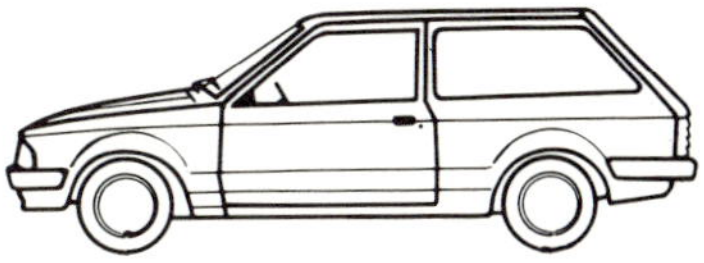

In the Driving Seat

Having found out a few details of the mechanics of the car, let's have a look at some of the more important things you'll need to know from the driving seat. The layout of all these models is pretty straightforward for the experienced motorist, but a little information on one or two things may be useful if you're not familiar with the car.

Instruments and controls

The accompanying illustrations show typical instrument panel layouts used on the various models. In general, all instruments, controls and switches are self-explanatory in their operation or function. However, it's as well to elaborate on some of these just to ensure their use is fully understood. It can be inconvenient, to say the least, if you've misinterpreted the reading of a certain gauge, or the flashing of one of the warning lights, having recently acquired or borrowed one of these vehicles.

Tachometer

This instrument records the engine speed by means of electrical impulses and is useful as a means of preventing over-revving of the engine in the intermediate gears. Note that it is only fitted to certain models.

Speedometer

This instrument's function is self-evident. It also incorporates a total mileage indicator. On certain models, a trip meter can be reset by means of the reset knob, and can be useful in checking the fuel consumption over a recorded mileage.

Fuel gauge and temperature gauge

The operation of the fuel gauge is self-evident. In addition a low fuel warning light is fitted to some models, details of which are given later in this Chapter.

The temperature gauge does not operate until the ignition is switched on. The gauges indicates the temperature of the coolant in the cooling system. Normally the needle should be around the centre of the scale once the engine is warmed up. Should the needle stay in the cool position after a few miles running, then this normally indicates that the thermostat in the cooling system is faulty and should be checked as soon as possible. If the needle enters the 'hot' sector, then the coolant is approaching or has reached boiling point and you should stop immediately to investigate the cause. Once again, a faulty thermostat is the most likely cause. Extra care must be taken when checking the coolant level when the engine is hot – see *Filling Station Facts* for the right way to do it.

Cigar lighter

To operate the cigar lighter, push the holder into the socket, then release it. When the lighter has

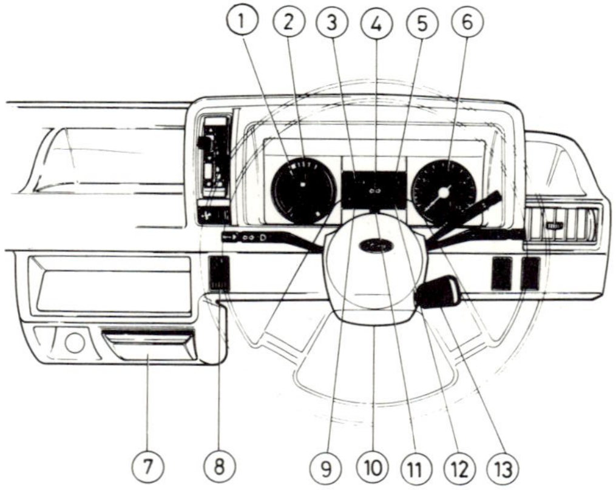

Instrument panel (base models)

1 Coolant temperature gauge
2 Fuel gauge
3 Handbrake 'on'/brake fluid warning lamp
4 Direction indicator warning lamp
5 Headlamp main beam warning lamp
6 Speedometer
7 Ashtray
8 Rear fog lamp switch
9 Oil pressure warning lamp
10 Bonnet release lever
11 Hazard warning flasher switch
12 Ignition warning lamp
13 Ignition switch/steering column lock

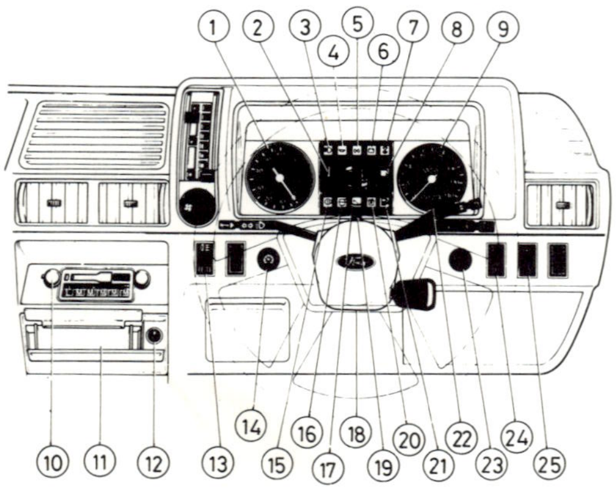

Instrument panel (top of the range models)

1 Tachometer (rev counter)
2 Coolant temperature gauge
3 Headlamp main beam warning lamp
4 Oil pressure warning lamp
5 Direction indicator warning lamp
6 Ignition warning lamp
7 Handbrake 'on'/brake fluid warning lamp
8 Fuel gauge
9 Speedometer
10 Radio
11 Ashtray
12 Cigar lighter
13 Rear fog lamp switch
14 Instrument illumination rheostat
15 Brake pad wear warning lamp
16 Low washer fluid level indicator lamp
17 Low engine oil level warning lamp
18 Bonnet release lever
19 Hazard warning switch
20 Low engine coolant level warning lamp
21 Low fuel level warning lamp
22 Mileage trip meter button
23 Windscreen wiper intermittent control
24 Heated rear window switch
25 Tailgate wash/wipe switch

reached the required temperature the holder will pop out to the extended position ready to use. It usually takes about fifteen seconds for the lighter to fully heat up. On some models, the cigar lighter is accessible only after the ashtray has been opened.

Transmission

The gearchange lever is floor-mounted. Forward speeds are simply selected by moving the lever to one of the desired gear positions, but reverse gear can only be engaged after the lever has been pushed downwards.

Heating and ventilation

The heating and ventilation system is operated by controls located in the centre of the facia panel.

Lever A controls the temperature (up – hot, down – cold) with variable settings in between.

Lever B controls the distribution of the air between screen (up) and vehicle interior (down). When the lever is *fully* down, air flow is shut off.

Switch C is the booster fan switch which may be of three-position rotary type or two-position toggle according to model.

The air entry through the louvred vents is controlled for direction and volume by means of the knurled wheel or moveable slats.

Stale air is extracted from slots in the rear edges of the doors.

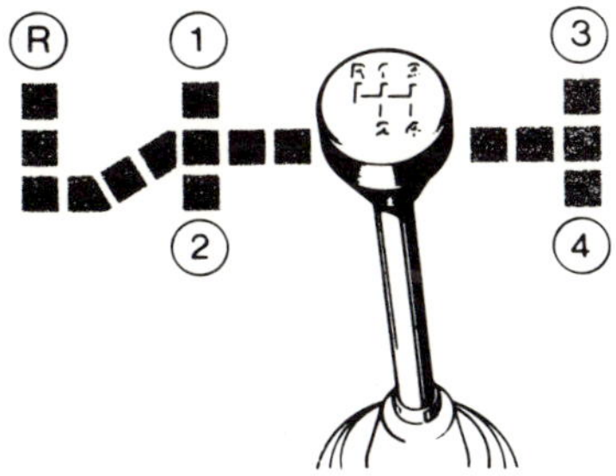

Gear lever positions (four-speed transmission)

Switches

Panel switches incorporate an amber coloured segment which gives a visual indication that the switch is on. When the vehicle lamps are switched on, the rocker switches are illuminated dimly for ease of location. This illumination intensifies in the particular switch which may be actuated.

Tailgate wash/wipe switch

To operate the wiper, depress the switch to the first position. To operate the washer, fully depress the switch with the finger and hold it down for as long a period as necessary.

Tailgate heated window switch

This will only operate when the ignition is switched on, and incorporates its own warning lamp. It is recommended that the operation of this device is limited to the period required for demisting, as the drain on the battery may be excessive when other electrical accessories are also in operation.

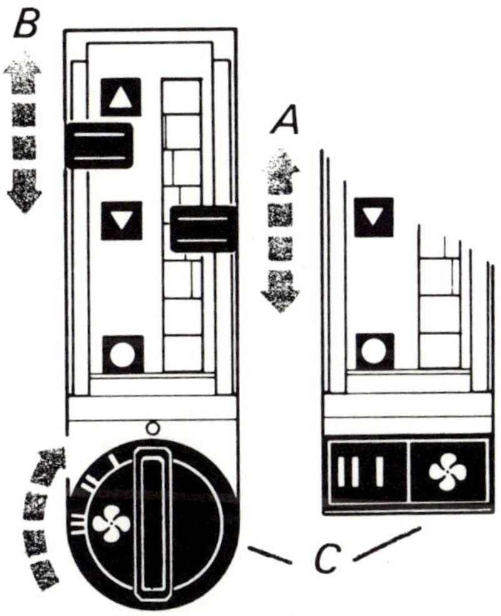

Heater controls

A Temperature control lever
B Air distribution lever
C Booster fan switch (alternative type)

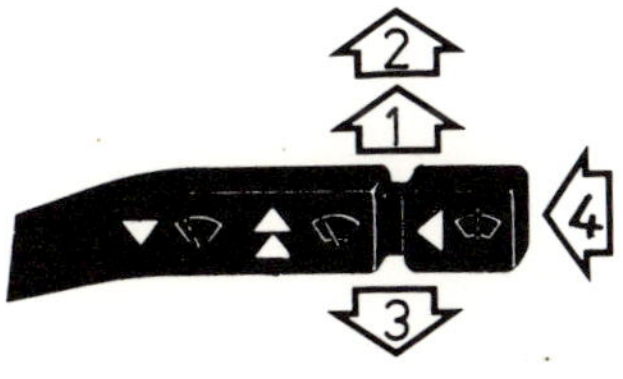

Windscreen wash/wipe switch

1 Normal speed
2 Fast speed
3 Single or intermittent wipe
4 Washers

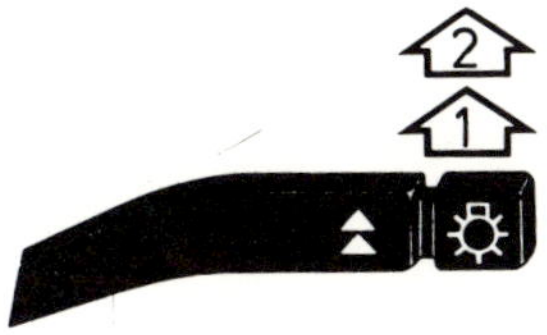

Lighting switch

1 Side and tail lamps
2 Headlamps

Multi-function switch

1 Horn
2 Right-hand indicator
3 Left-hand indicator
4 Headlamp main beam
5 Headlamp flasher

Windscreen wiper intermittent operation control switch

The interval between the wiping phases can be varied by turning the control knob clockwise to increase the length of the interval or anti-clockwise to reduce it.

Hazard flasher switch

The hazard warning lamps will operate once the switch is depressed, irrespective of whether the ignition is on or off.

Rear fog lamp switch

This switch incorporates its own warning lamp and will only operate if the ignition is on and the headlamps are switched to the dipped beam position.

Windscreen wash/wipe switch

This is of stalk type mounted on the right-hand side of the steering column. Its functions are as follows:
Up – position 1: normal wiper speed
Up – position 2: fast wiper speed
Down – position 3: single or intermittent wipe
Depress – position 4: washer operation. On models equipped with headlamp washers, these will operate as well provided the headlamps are switched on.

Lighting switch

This is also mounted on the right-hand side of the steering column. Its functions are as follows:
Up – position 1: side and tail lamps on
Up – position 2: headlamps, side and tail lamps on

Multi-function switch

This switch is mounted on the left-hand side of the steering column, and functions as follows:
Up – position 2: right-hand indicator
Down – position 3: left-hand indicator
Forward – position 4: headlamp main beam
Back – position 5: headlamp flasher
Depress – position 1: horn

Ignition switch/steering lock

The ignition switch/steering lock has four positions as shown. Their functions are as follows:

With the key in position O, the steering is locked and the ignition is switched off. *Under no circumstances should the key be returned to this position when the vehicle is in motion, as it will be impossible to steer the vehicle, with consequent disastrous results!*

With the key in position I, the steering is unlocked but the ignition remains switched off. However, in this position it is possible to operate any accessories wired to work independently of the ignition (eg radio or cassette player).

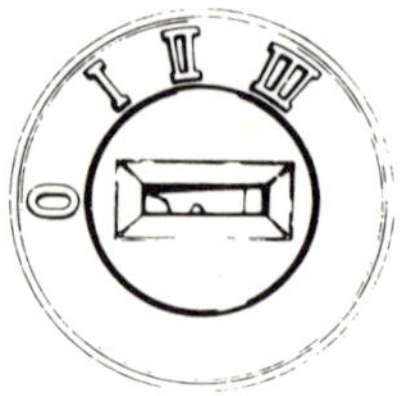

Ignition switch/steering lock key positions

O   Ignition off, steering locked
I   Ignition off, accessories on, steering unlocked
II   Ignition on
III   Start engine (repeat operation only after returning key to position I)

With the key in position II the ignition and all other circuits are switched on for normal running.

With the key in position III the starter motor is operated. Note that if the engine does not start once the starter motor has been operated, the key must be returned to position I before it will operate again.

There are two final points to note. The first is that to unlock the steering from position O, it will be necessary to depress the key and lock barrel slightly into the lock before the key will turn. It may also be necessary to move the steering wheel slightly to release the tension on the lock. The second point is that if the vehicle is being towed, the key should be in position II so that the steering is unlocked and the stop lights and indicators function.

Instrument panel illuminating switch

This switch is of the rheostat type and rotation of the switch knob will vary the brightness of the illumination.

Warning lamps

A number of warning lamps are located on the instrument panel. Should a warning lamp come on during normal motoring, take immediate action where applicable to find the cause and rectify matters. Warning lamps cover the following functions:

Oil (low) pressure
Direction indicator
Ignition warning (no charge)
Headlamp main beam
Handbrake 'on' and low brake fluid level
*Low fuel level**
*Low engine coolant**
*Low engine oil level (ohc only)**
*Low washer fluid level**
*Disc pad wear**

The lamps marked with an asterisk are only fitted to certain models and where they are installed, they form part of an auxiliary warning system. When the ignition is first switched on, all the system warning lamps will illuminate for a five second period to verify that all the bulbs are working satisfactorily. After the five second check, all lights should extinguish to indicate that the levels checked are satisfactory.

If a light remains on, a low level has been registered, and that particular item should be checked and the necessary action taken.

If a light flashes on and off for about 40 seconds, a fault in the checking circuit is indicated, and the particular item should be checked visually.

The check for the oil level only functions at initial start-up, and becomes inoperative with the engine running. When running, the oil pressure is monitored by the main oil warning light. The oil level check will not function again until approximately three minutes after the engine was last run.

The purpose of most warning and indicator lamps is self-evident, but one or two require a rather more detailed description.

Ignition warning light

This serves the dual purpose of reminding the driver that the ignition circuit is switched on (even though the engine may not be running), as well as acting as a no-charge indicator. It should light up when the ignition is switched on, and may also be on when the engine is idling, but should go out at any engine speed above idling. If this doesn't happen, you've probably got a problem on your hands which needs pretty urgent attention.

Oil pressure warning light

This light should only be on when the ignition is switched on, and should go out as soon as the engine is running. If it doesn't go out within a second or so of start-up, it suggests that a considerable degree of wear exists somewhere in the engine, or (less likely) that some of the oilways are blocked. These faults can be lived with for a while, but expect problems in the not too distant future! If the warning light comes on while you're travelling, *switch off the engine immediately.* It could be a duff switch, but more likely you're out of oil or the lubrication system has failed, and that's serious. If you can't find the cause, get expert assistance – but don't drive the car.

Fuel level warning light

In addition to the fuel gauge, a warning light is fitted to alert the driver that the fuel level is getting particularly low. This will start to illuminate (perhaps intermittently at first) when the tank content is down to approximately $1\frac{1}{2}$ gallons (7.0 litres).

Handbrake 'on' and low brake fluid level warning light

With the ignition switched on, this warning lamp will come on whenever the handbrake is applied.

Should the lamp come on during driving, first check that the handbrake is fully released; if it is, then the fluid level is dangerously low due to lack of topping up or a leak in the hydraulic system. The cause must be ascertained and rectified immediately.

Miscellaneous

Door locks and childproof catches

A front door may be locked by closing it and then turning the key in the cylinder lock. Alternatively, with the door open, depress the lock interior plunger knob and then close the door, making sure to keep the exterior handle fully raised during closure. To lock a rear door, hold the door open, depress the lock interior plunger knob and close the door.

On five-door models, the rear door locks incorporate a childproof catch to prevent the doors from being opened from the inside when children are

Rear door childproof lock lever

being carried. To operate this facility, push the small lever on the door edge downwards.

All doors can of course be locked from the inside by simply depressing the lock plunger knobs.

Central door locking system

This is available as an option and provides remote control locking and unlocking of doors and tailgate on three- or five-door models. By using the key in the lock on the driver's door or by operating the interior plunger on this door, all other doors and the tailgate are automatically locked or unlocked.

With a control locking system, it is still possible to operate all the door and tailgate locks independently. A circuit breaker is located at the fusebox to prevent overloading.

Electrically operated front windows

This is another option available on most hatchback models. The electric motor drivegear engages directly with the window regulator mechanism, and takes over the function of the winder handle used on manually operated windows.

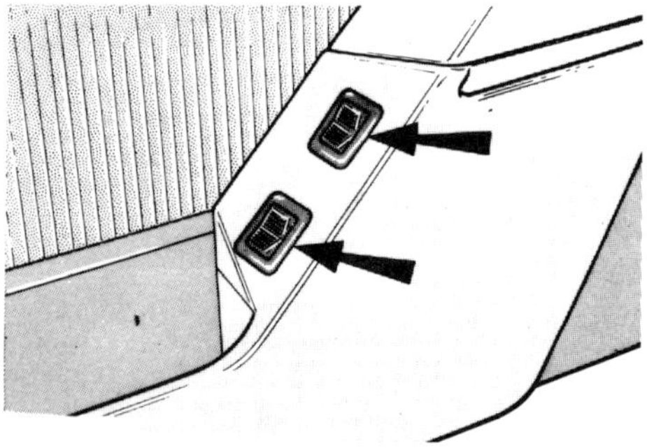

Electric window switches (driver's side shown)

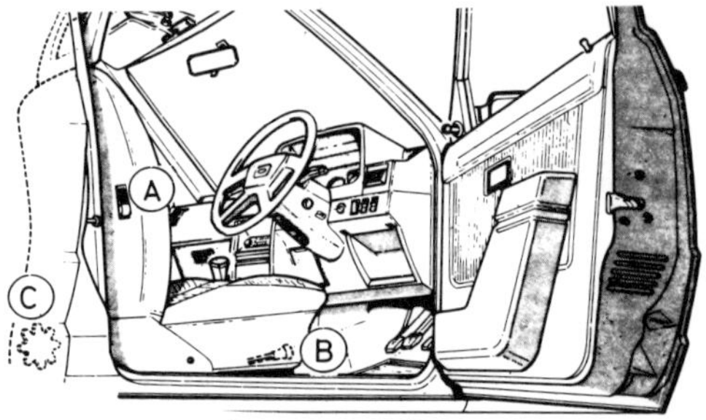

Front seat adjusters

A Seat back release lever (3-door models)
B Seat slide lever
C Seat back reclining control wheel

When the ignition is switched on, power is supplied through a relay mounted in the fusebox. When a control switch is actuated, the motor operates to lower or raise the window. A circuit breaker type of overload protection is provided in the event of a window being obstructed for some reason – the circuit breaker is in the fusebox.

The control switches are of the rocker type and are mounted in the front door armrests. There's a single switch operating the passenger's window in the passenger's door armrest. At the driver's side two switches are provided, one for the passenger's window, the other for the driver's window. Depressing the lower end of the rocker switch causes the window to be lowered, depressing the top end of the switch raises it.

Bonnet release mechanism

The bonnet catch is released by pulling the lever which is located under the steering column shroud. The safety catch now visible between the grille panel and bonnet can then be released by pressing the lever upwards to disengage the catch hook. The bonnet can then be raised and supported by the stay provided. Ensure the stay is properly located in the bonnet slot, or you may find the bonnet descending towards your head at a somewhat rapid speed!

Interior lamp

This is located above the windscreen and incorporates a three-position switch: on, off, and courtesy lamp function in conjunction with the plunger type switches on the door edges.

Seats

The position of the front seats may be adjusted by moving the slide lever under the front of the seat towards the right-hand side. Slide the seat in its runners to the desired position and make sure that the adjustment lever 'clicks' positively into its locking notch on completion.

The seat back inclination is adjustable by means of the handwheel provided.

On three-door versions, a seat back release lever

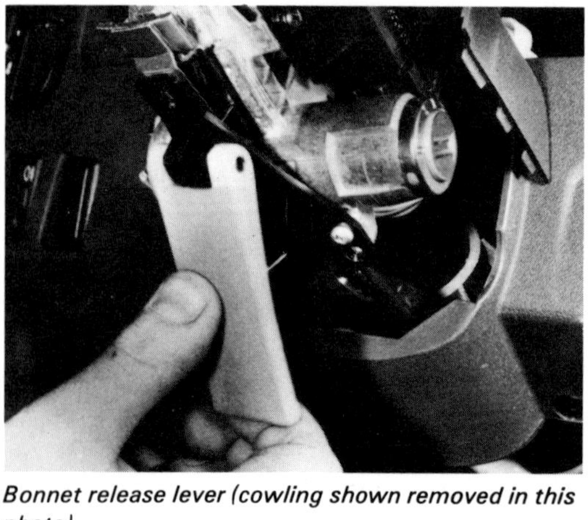

Bonnet release lever (cowling shown removed in this photo)

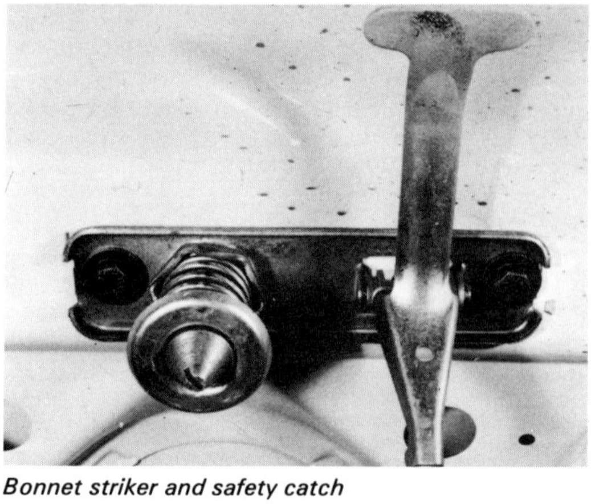

Bonnet striker and safety catch

is provided so that the seat back can be tilted forward to make access to the rear seats easier.

Converting rear compartment load floor

On both the hatchback and estate models, the rear seat folds flat to give the maximum load carrying area. Pull the rear of the seat cushion forward using the strap provided. Detach the supporting cords and lift out the rear parcels tray. Release the levers, one at each side of the seat back. On five-door versions, slightly open both rear doors to prevent the door armrests from obstructing the seat back as it is folded forward.

Where the vehicle is equipped with rear seat belts, guide them carefully round the seat back when it is being moved. Take care not to trap the centre lap belt under the seat cushion as it is returned to its usual position for passenger carrying.

Sunroof

The sunroof panel may be slid open or closed or its rear edge tilted upwards.

To open or close the panel, ease the winder from its storage recess and turn it in an anti-clockwise direction to open or clockwise to close.

To tilt the roof panel, turn the window control clockwise, overriding the resistance felt at the fully closed position. If the roof panel is to be tilted when the vehicle is travelling at high speed, it is recommended that the facia side vents are first opened to counteract any vacuum effects.

Multi-function digital clock

This type of clock is fitted to certain models only. It is located immediately above the interior mirror in a unit with the courtesy light. It will show the time in hours and minutes, the date, and elapsed time when used as a stopwatch.

The clock normally displays the time with ignition switched on, with the colon between hours and minutes flashing on once a second. Depressing the function button once displays the date and month for a four second period, after which the display reverts back to the time function.

To set the time, the ignition should be switched on. Depression of the upper recessed button with a ballpoint pen will show the hour followed by 'A' or 'P' signifying 'am' or 'pm'. The hour will be advanced by one each time the button is again depressed. Four seconds after the button was last operated, the time display returns with the newly set hour number. Depression of the lower recessed button in similar fashion is used to set the minutes. The clock will have been stopped at this point (colon not flashing) and depression of the stop/start button is required to activate it again.

Multi-function digital clock controls

1 Upper recessed setting button
2 Lower recessed setting button
3 Function button
4 Display
5 Reset button (for elapsed time function)
6 Stop/start button

The date and month display is set as follows. Depress the function button once to bring up the calendar display. Depression of the upper recessed button immediately after this changes the day number as previously described for time. The month number is set in similar fashion using the lower recessed button. Four seconds after the last depression of either button, the display returns to show normal time. Note that the calendar adjusts itself to allow for the different number of days in each month, except for the month of February in a leap year. In this case manual adjustment is required.

It will be seen that the clock display is blank with the ignition switched off. The time will be displayed for a few seconds on depression of the function button once. Depression of this button twice brings up the date for a few seconds. Note that it is not possible to reset either of these functions with the ignition switched off.

The clock has a quick time set function. This enables small corrections to be made without using the recessed setting buttons. When the clock reads 58, 59, 00 or 01 minutes, it can be reset to 00 minutes 00 seconds by pressing the stop/start button once. For 58 and 59 minutes, the hour number is advanced by one, for 00 and 01 minutes the hour number remains unchanged.

For those interested, the clock also incorporates an elapsed timer function. An explanation of the ins and outs of its operation would be fairly lengthy and is considered beyond the scope of this Handbook. We suggest you contact your local dealer or refer to the driver's handbook supplied with the car if necessary.

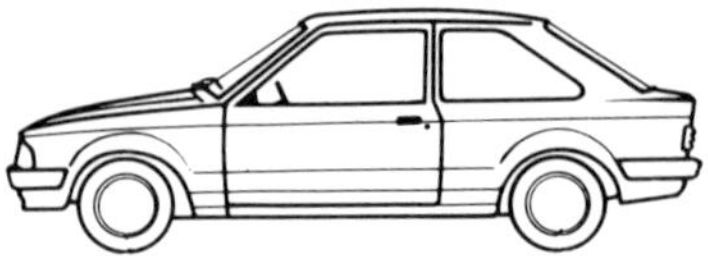

Filling Station Facts

Forgetting about the actual servicing and mechanical maintenance of your car for the time being, there are some things which are so simple they're likely to get overlooked: but they're not only an important part of the maintenance of your car – they're vital for its safety and reliability too. Three of these items – tyres, oil and water – you can check if necessary whenever you visit a petrol station. We've set out here the absolute minimum of information you need right from the very first day you drive your Escort.

Topping up oil

Whenever you top up the oil level, always try to use the same grade and brand; and do avoid using cheap oil – the initial saving will probably be lost in increased engine wear over a prolonged period – or perhaps a short one!

When checking the oil level, ensure that the car's standing on level ground. Take out the dipstick, wipe it clean, then refit it fully. Pull it out again and note the oil level. Under no circumstances should the level be allowed to drop below the 'MIN' mark on the dipstick. Add oil as necessary to bring the level to the 'MAX' mark on the dipstick. Avoid overfilling, and mop up any oil which may have been spilt.

On models fitted with an auxiliary warning system (low engine oil level warning lamp) take care that the leads and the multi-plug are not disturbed as the dipstick is withdrawn.

Checking coolant level

This can be done visually by observing the level of coolant in the radiator expansion tank when cold. This should be between the 'MIN' and 'MAX' marks on the tank. During normal operation, the addition of coolant will seldom, if ever, be required, but if it is, always add it by pouring into the expansion tank – never into the thermostat housing.

On ohv engines, coolant expansion is taken care of by a pressure relief valve on the cap of the thermostat housing. This allows coolant to pass through an overflow tube into the expansion tank. As the system cools and coolant is drawn back into the system, the vacuum valve also incorporated in the cap opens to prevent a vacuum condition occurring.

On CVH engines, the expansion tank is of 'degas' type and the necessary pressure/vacuum relief valve is incorporated in the tank cap.

If the engine is hot, do not be tempted to release the cap on the thermostat housing (ohv engine) or expansion tank (CVH engine) unless it's absolutely necessary, as the sudden release of pressure may cause scalding. If you find that you *have* to remove

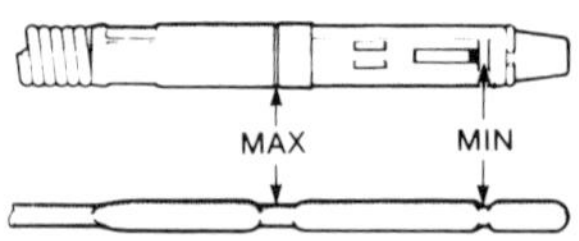

Types of dipstick markings

Topping up engine oil

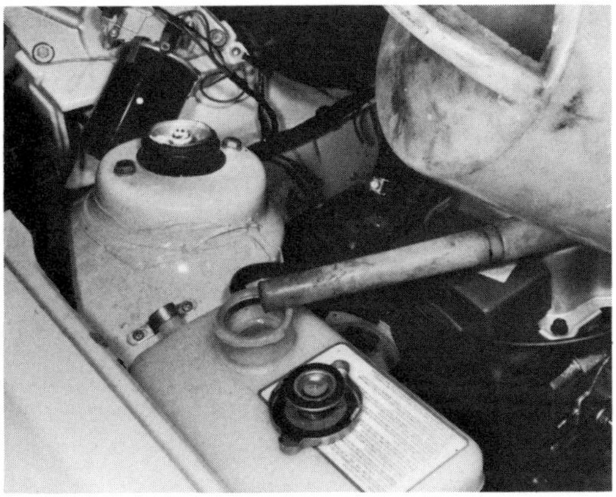
Topping up coolant expansion tank (CVH engine)

Checking a tyre pressure

the cap with the engine hot for any reason, *take care to avoid scalding* – protect your hands with thick rag and loosen the cap a little at a time until any pressure has been released.

Always top up with the mixture of antifreeze and water of the same strength as that already in the system. You can use plain water if you're stuck, but don't make a habit of it or you'll dilute the antifreeze remaining in the system.

If the cooling system does require frequent topping up, check for external leaks at the radiator and connecting hoses. If none is found, the leakage may be due to an internal fault such as a blown cylinder head gasket or crack in the cylinder head or block. This can sometimes be verified by a sudden apparent rise in the engine oil level or quantities of water being ejected from the exhaust pipe after starting the engine.

Due to the light alloy cylinder head construction and high operating temperatures of the ohc engine, it is imperative that anti-freeze mixture conforming to Ford Specification SS-M97B-9103-A and of specified strength is always used in the cooling system if severe corrosion is to be avoided. The specified strength is 45% antifreeze 55% water.

Checking tyre pressures

When checking tyre pressures don't forget to check the pressure in the spare – in the event of a puncture you could be in for a 'let down'! If you're wise enough to have your own tyre pressure gauge, always use this to check the pressures – garage gauges aren't always terribly accurate and it's essential that the pressures are right to ensure the correct handling of the car when steering and braking.

Remember that tyre pressures can only be checked accurately when the tyres are cold. Any tyre that's travelled more than a mile or so will show a pressure increase of several pounds per square inch (psi) – maybe more than 5 psi after a longer run. So a certain amount of 'guesstimation' comes into checking tyres if they're warm.

Since the pressures won't increase for any reason other than heat, the least you can do is to ensure that the pressures in the two front tyres are equal, bearing in mind that they may be a bit above these shown in the table. (The same applies to the two back tyres, but remember that their pressures may be different from the front).

If one tyre of a pair has a low pressure when hot, bring it up to the pressure of the other at the same end of the car. If they're both below the recommended cold pressure although warm, the safest thing to do is to bring them up to about 3 psi above it, to allow for cooling.

With the tyres properly inflated, run your hand

and eyes over the tyre walls and tread. This is best done with the wheel off the ground so that it can be rotated but, if you're really not feeling up to it, move the car backwards and forwards a foot or two, so that you can check all round. The tread depth must not be less than 1 mm over at least three-quarters of the width, and around the full circumference. You can buy gauges for checking this, but a 2p piece inserted in the tread groove is a good guide. If the tread's not deeper than the distance from the row of dots to the edge of the coin, you're breaking the law, so get some replacements pretty quickly. There must also be no cuts, bulges or other deformities; if these are present, you're also breaking the law.

Self-service garages

More and more garages now operate on a self-service basis so that the customer's subjected to the intricacies of refueling his or her own vehicle. Regulars to this type of establishment need no introduction to its methods of operation and can usually be seen going through the routine at high speed like well-oiled robots. To the newcomer, the operation of the various kinds of pump can at first be confusing, but don't panic! Carefully read each instruction on the pump in turn before attempting to work it.

Depending upon the fuel tank venting arrangement of a particular car, sometimes it is best to insert the pump delivery nozzle fully into the tank filler neck, while on others to only just insert the nozzle, so giving trapped air a better chance to escape. Experience will guide you as to the best method, but in any event, try to regulate the fuel flow at an even rate so that it's not too fast. All pumps now have an automatic flowback valve mechanism fitted in them, which prevents any surplus petrol making a speedy exit from the filler neck all over the unsuspecting operator. On completion, don't forget to refit your petrol filler cap!

QUICK CHECK CHART

TYRE PRESSURES COLD	
Up to 3 occupants:	
Front	26 psi (1.8 bar)
Rear	26 psi (1.8 bar)
Fully laden:	
Front	28 psi (2.0 bar)
Rear	33 psi (2.3 bar)
FUEL TANK CAPACITY	8.8 gal (40 litres)
FUEL GRADE	4 star (min 97 octane)
ENGINE OIL TYPE	Multigrade SAE 20W-50
QUANTITY OF OIL REQUIRED TO BRING LEVEL FROM 'MIN' TO 'MAX' ON DIPSTICK	1.75 pints (1.0 litre)

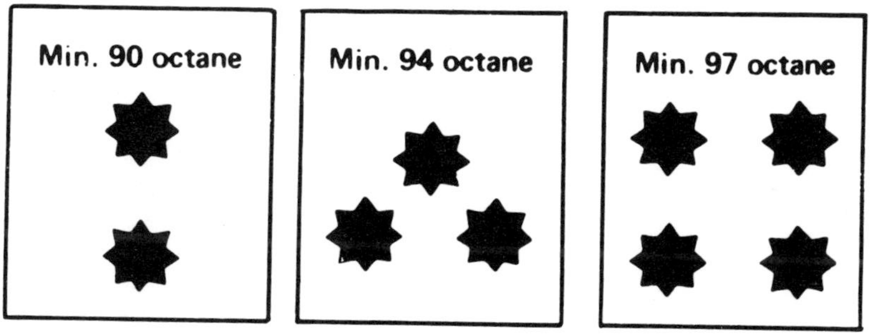

Fuel octane star rating symbols – use the correct grade for your model

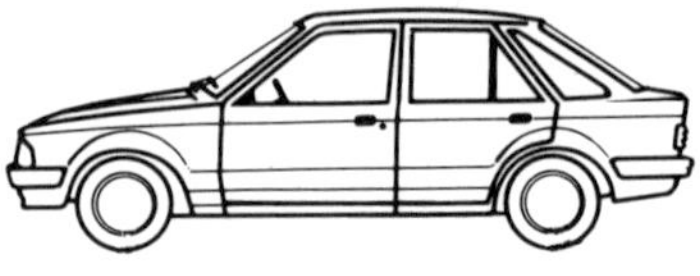

In an Emergency

A car hasn't been invented yet that can guarantee you a safe and reliable journey from A to B every day of your life. Be it due to a breakdown or a puncture, the day will come when your trusty transport requires a bit of roadside attention – usually at the most inconvenient time. In this Handbook you'll find a wealth of information which should certainly minimise the possibility of a breakdown but, although we hope it won't be very often, the odd thing is bound to go wrong from time to time.

The *Troubleshooter* Section should help to trace the cause of an unexpected problem, but it's not much good knowing what's wrong if you've nothing to put it right with, or needing to change a wheel in the dark when you haven't a clue how the jack works. A few timely minutes spent reading through this Chapter now could save your time and temper later on!

Spares and repairs kit

The tool kit supplied with the car is the basic requirement to change a wheel with and nothing more. When a breakdown occurs other than a puncture you will therefore be stuck unless you have taken the precaution of carrying a few spare parts and some tools along in the luggage compartment. Now, whilst it is not practicable to motor around carrying a vast quantity of spares and a full range of tools, a few of the more basic requirement can easily be carried and may well get you mobile again. Tool requirements are discussed in *Tools for the Job,* and of course the tools carried can also be used for servicing the car.

A few items which can be used or fitted without too much bother at the roadside should also be carried. These can prove invaluable in getting you out of trouble on the odd occasion when they might be needed. The sort of things you should carry are:

Spark plug, clean with correct gap

HT lead and plug cap – long enough to reach the plug furthest from the distributor

Set of main light bulbs

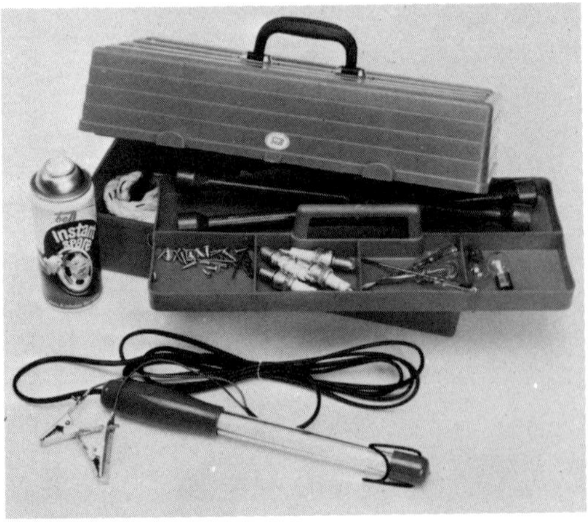

A box like this is useful for keeping your emergency repair kit together

An *'Instant Spare' aerosol in use on a flat tyre*

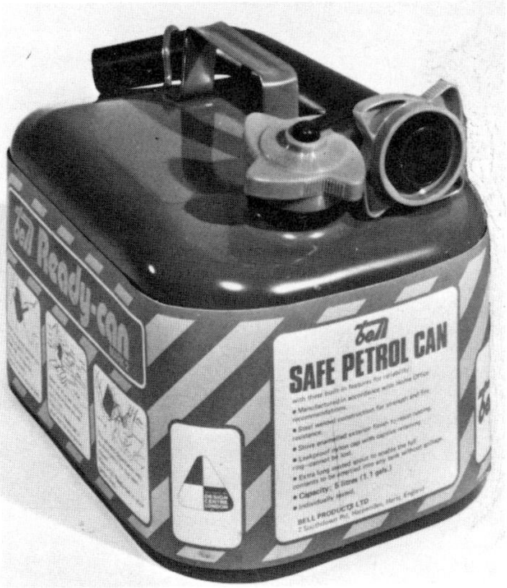

If you want to carry emergency petrol, use an approved safety can of the type shown here. The detachable spout makes pouring easy, too

Pocket tyre pressure gauge
Spare fuses
Distributor rotor, condenser and contact points (where applicable)
Alternator drivebelt
Roll of insulating tape
Tin of radiator sealer and a hose bandage
Extension light and lead with crocodile clips, or a good torch
Clean lint-free cloth
Breakdown triangle
Tow rope
First aid box
Spare set of keys (but not kept in the car)
De-icer aerosol (during winter)
This Handbook or Haynes Workshop Manual

Of course, it's possible to expand this list indefinitely; for example, you might prefer to have a set of spare coolant hoses instead of just a repair bandage, but obviously there has to be a compromise or you'll have no spare room in the back!

We'll mention here just three other items for emergency use which it might make you feel happier to have on board. The first is a 'universal' temporary fanbelt which can be fitted without loosening any bolts and which will enable you to get going again quickly in the event of a belt breakage, and to fit a proper replacement belt at your leisure.

The second 'get-you-home' device is an instant puncture repair in the form of an aerosol can. The nozzle is screwed on to the tyre valve, and releases sealant to seal the leak, together with gas to reinflate the tyre. It's suitable for tubed or tubeless tyres and will at the very least allow you to drive to a garage without getting your hands dirty.

If you want to carry an extra gallon of petrol for emergencies, use one of the safety cans now on the market. They're not only specially constructed to be safe in an accident and to prevent leakage, but they're so much easier to pour from than something like an old oil can.

Flat battery

Apart from old age (average life expectancy 3 years), a battery will normally only go flat if the charging circuit is defective, as indicated by a continuously glowing ignition warning light, or when a particular circuit (headlights for example) is left on for an indefinite period with the engine switched off.

To start a car with a flat battery you can either have it pushed or towed and with 2nd gear engaged let in the clutch, or if jump leads are available, connect up your battery to one that is fully charged. If the latter course of action is to be taken, *two important points must be observed* The first is to ensure that the leads are correctly interconnected with + (positive) to + and – (negative) to –. The second is not to allow the bodies of the two cars to touch. As soon as your engine has started, keep it running at a fast tickover and detach the jump leads. If towing the vehicle to start it, observe the notes given later in this Chapter.

Jacking and wheel changing

The jack supplied in the vehicle tool kit should only be used for emergency roadside wheel changing, unless it is supplemented with axle stands. Use the jack at the mounting points on either side of the vehicle just below the sill.

To begin the wheel changing operation, first apply the handbrake firmly and engage first or reverse gear; then find something to chock the wheels on the other side of the car. An old brick or block of wood is just the job, but unless you carry such a thing you may have to improvise. If you can only find one, weigh up which way the car's likely to move if anything goes wrong; hopefully you'll find two, then one can be put each side of a wheel.

Before lifting the car, but with the jack engaged in its socket, loosen (but do not remove) the four roadwheel retaining bolts. If the bolts were last

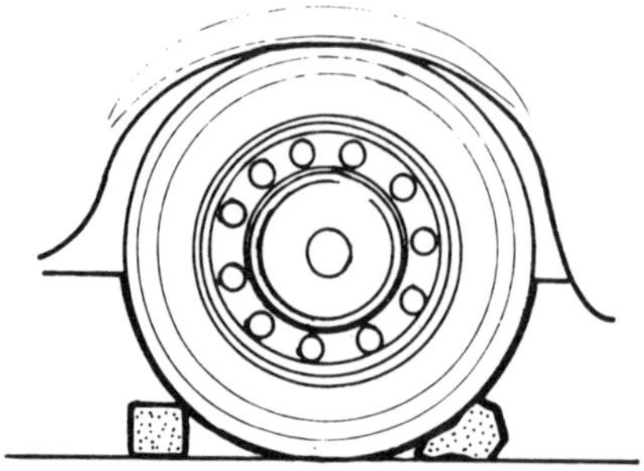

Always wedge the wheels before jacking

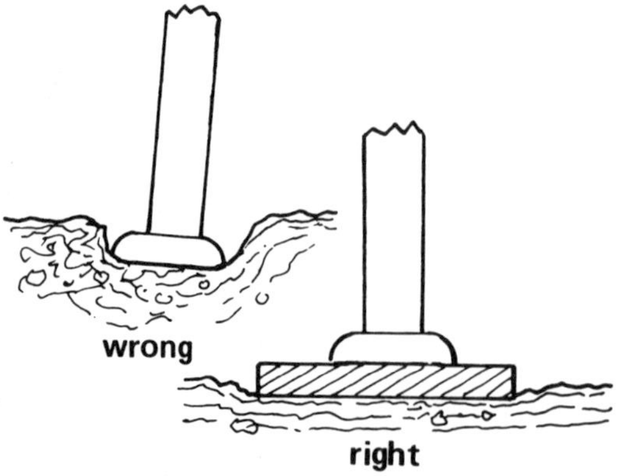

Spread the load under the foot of the jack

Spare wheel with anchor bolt

Car jack stowed in spare wheel

Sill jacking location

tightened by a garage or a tyre fitting depot using an air-operated wrench, they may be very tight, in which case a length of piping or box spanner pushed onto the angled wrench supplied in the tool kit will provide the extra leverage needed to unscrew them.

The car can now be raised, but make sure it doesn't move and check that the chocks are still in position. Unscrew the bolts and then remove the wheel.

Fit the spare wheel to the car and pinch up the bolts in a crosswise order, then lower the car to the ground. Fully tighten the bolts – you don't have to stand on the wrench to do this, but make sure they're good and tight.

If you're following the correct service procedures, the spare will have plenty of pressure in it; if necessary let it down to the correct reading by pressing in the pin in the centre of the valve to release air, and checking with your pressure gauge. If it hasn't got enough pressure, make a mental note to keep it checked in future and drive carefully to the nearest air-line, or use your own foot or hand pump.

Towing and being towed

Tow rope connections must be made to the towing hooks of the vehicle and not to the bumper bars or brackets. Make sure that any tow rope being used is of sufficient length, and remember that without the engine running, the power assistance for the brakes won't be available and harder foot pressure will therefore be required. Always unlock the steering column if being towed by another vehicle.

Maintenance of lights

Remember that a defective exterior light can be not only dangerous but also illegal. Carrying spare bulbs will enable you to renew blown ones as they occur. A failed interior lamp or panel light bulb may be

Front towing eye

Rear towing eye

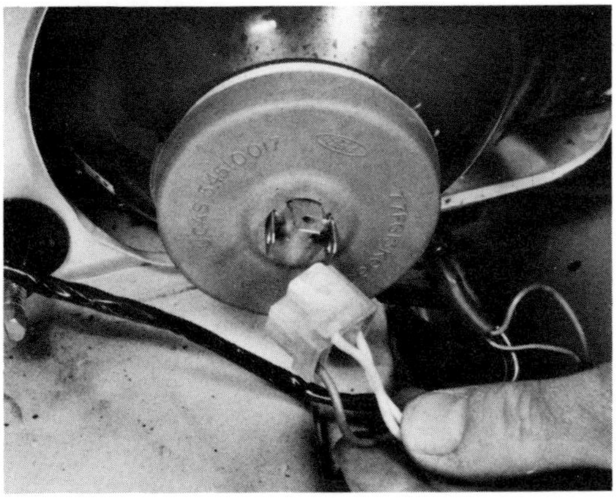

Headlamp plug

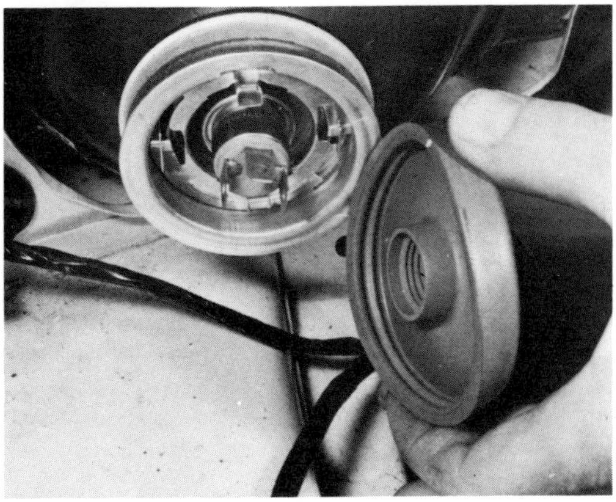

Headlamp rubber cover

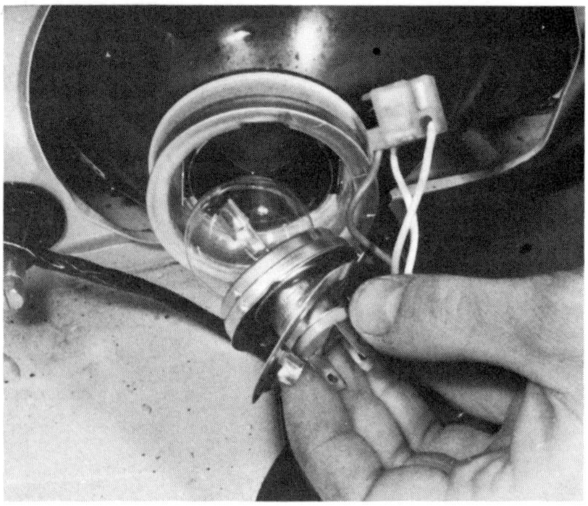

Removing headlamp bulb

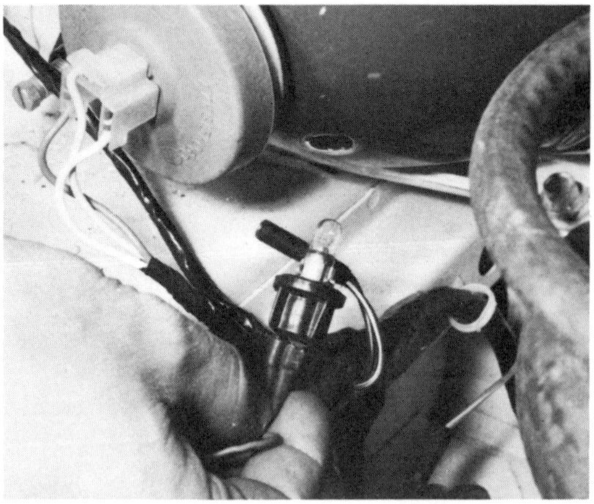

Parking lamp bulb

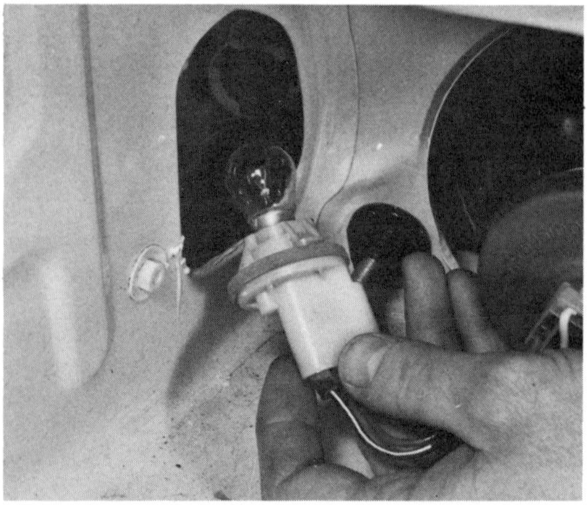

Front indicator bulb

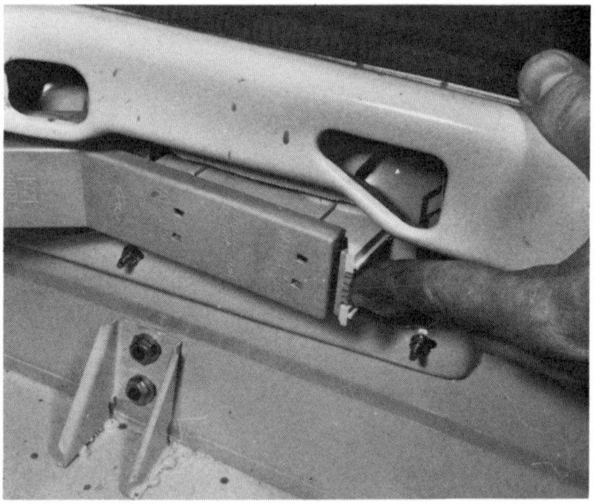

Releasing rear lamp cluster

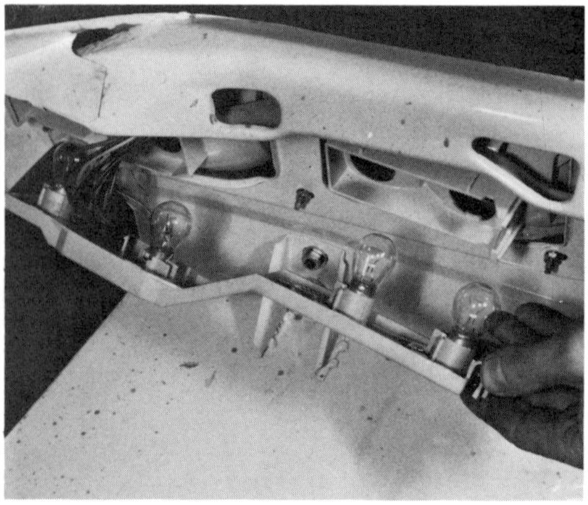

Rear lamp bulb holder

Rear number plate lamp

just a nuisance, but an exterior lamp could be a life or death matter. Blown bulbs can be renewed as follows.

Headlamp

To change a headlamp bulb, first of all open the bonnet. Working inside the engine compartment, pull the multi-plug from the rear of the headlamp. Remove the rubber gaiter and rotate the bulb securing clip or extract the spring clip, according to type. The duff bulb can now be withdrawn. Fit the new bulb, avoiding handling it with the fingers. If you have touched it, wipe the bulb with a pad moistened in methylated spirit.

Front parking lamp

The operations are similar to those just described for the headlamp bulb. Twist the parking lamp bulb holder from the headlamp unit.

Front indicator lamp

Working inside the engine compartment, twist the bulb holder from the rear of the lamp, then remove the bulb from the holder.

Auxiliary lamp and foglamp

Remove the single lens securing screw, pull the lens/reflector forward and disconnect the lead from the spade terminal. Release the bulb holder retaining clip and take out the bulb. Do not handle a bulb with the fingers, but if the glass is touched, clean it with a pad moistened in methylated spirit.

Rear lamps

Car: Open the tailgate, depress the catch on the bulb holder and pull it from its location. Now remove the bulb from its holder.

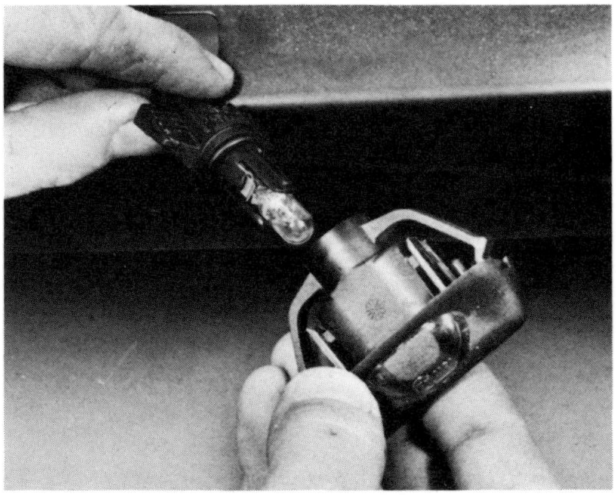

Rear number plate lamp bulb

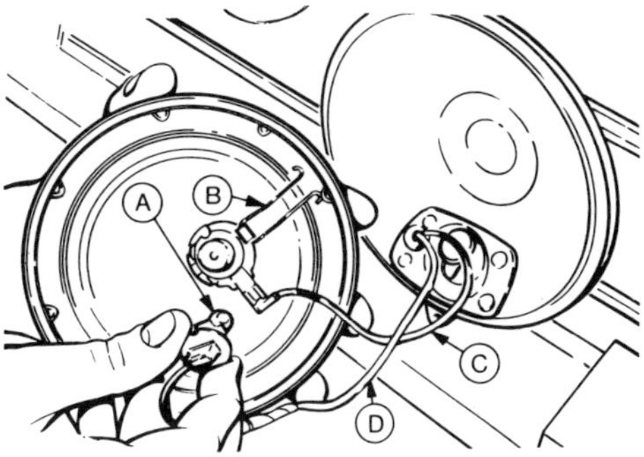

Auxiliary lamp bulb holder

C Earth wire
D Feed wire
A Bulb
B Clip

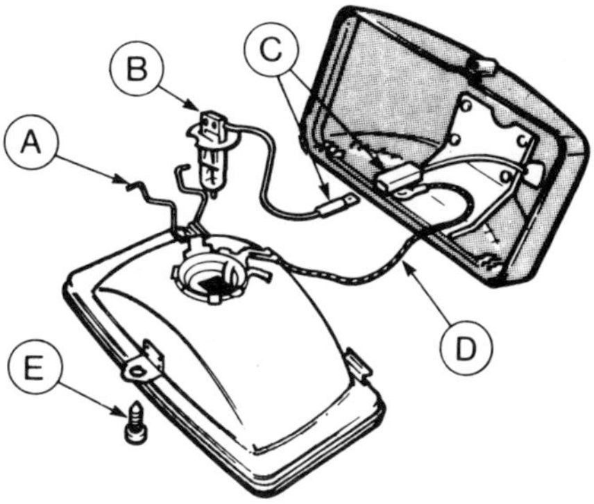

Foglamp bulb holder

A Bulb clip
B Bulb
C Connector
D Earth wire
E Lens screw

Estate: Open the tailgate and remove the rear trim panel. Release the bulb holder by pressing one clip up and the other one down with the thumbs, then remove the bulb.

Rear number plate lamp

Reach under the rear bumper and disconnect the wiring multiplug. Squeeze the tangs which retain the lamp to the bumper, pull and remove. The base of the lamp contains the bulb which is removed by gently pulling.

Side repeater lamp

Release the lamp from the wing by reaching up under the wing and squeezing the lamp retaining tangs. Push out the lamp and twist the bulb holder from it in an anticlockwise direction. Pull the bulb gently from its holder.

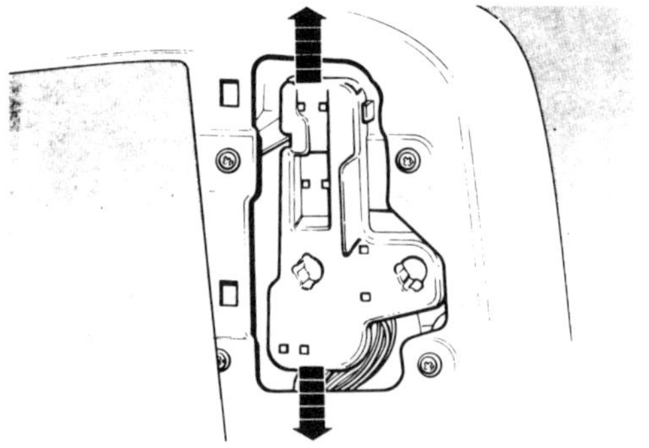

Rear lamp bulb holder (Estate)

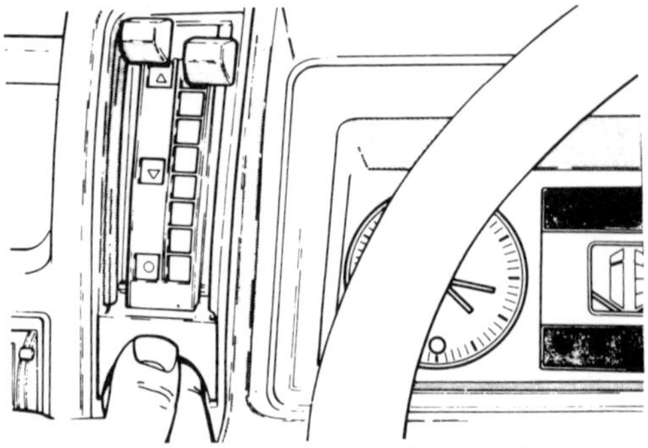

Removing heater control panel trim

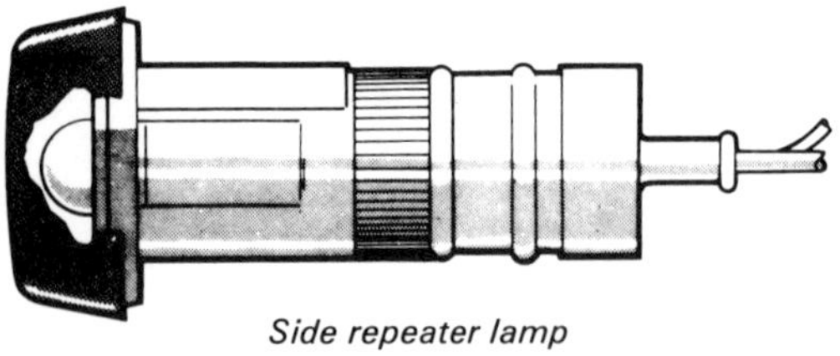

Side repeater lamp

Hazard warning switch bulb and cover

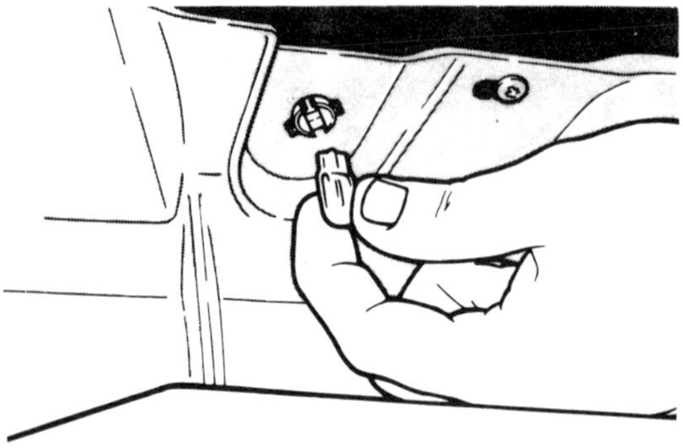

Removing glove compartment lamp bulb

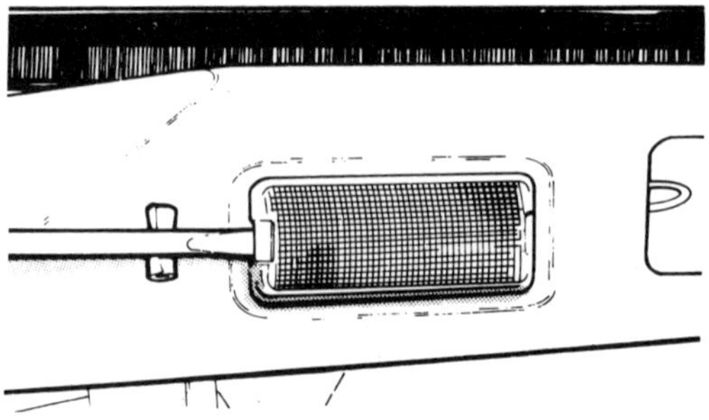

Prising out luggage compartment lamp

Glove compartment lamp

This is simply a matter of gently pulling the bulb from its holder.

Heater control illumination lamp

Slide the heater control levers to the top of their travel. Pull off the heater motor switch knob and then unclip the control trim panel from the facia. Pull the bulb from the lamp socket.

Hazard warning switch

Grip the switch cover and pull it off. Gently pull the bulb from its socket.

Interior front lamp

Carefully prise the lamp from its location and remove the bulb from its spring contact on the lamp body.

Luggage compartment lamp

Using a thin screwdriver, prise the lamp from its location. Remove the bulb from its spring contact clip.

Fuses, relays and circuit breakers

These are combined in one box under the bonnet. The fuses are numbered to identify the circuit which

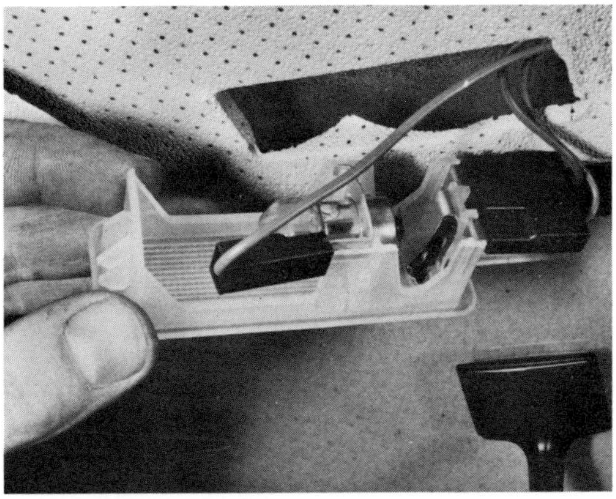

Interior (courtesy) lamp

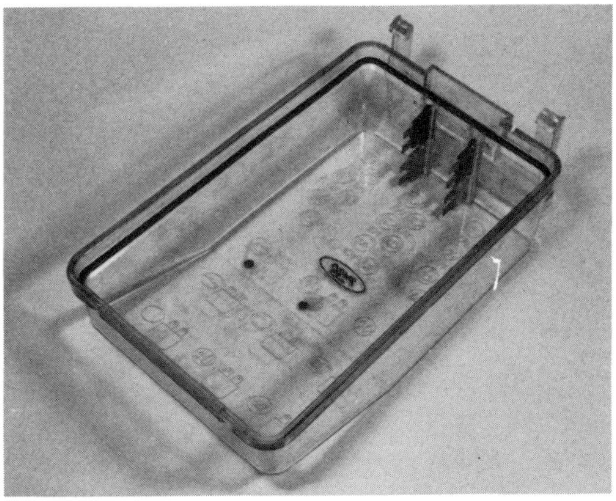

Fusebox cover

they protect, and the circuits are represented by symbols on the plastic cover of the box.

When an accessory or other electrical component or system fails, always check the fuse first. The fuses are coloured red (10A), blue (15A) or yellow (20/25A). Never replace a fuse with one of higher rating or bypass it with tinfoil, and if the new fuse blows immediately, check the reason before renewing again. The most common cause of a fuse blowing is faulty insulation creating a short-circuit. Spare fuses are carried in the fusebox lid.

Relays are of the plug-in type and are used for the following circuits (as applicable):

Auxiliary foglamp
Heated rear window
Auxiliary driving lamp
Direction indicators
Headlamp washer
Windscreen wiper delay
Ignition relay

Circuit breakers are only fitted to vehicles equipped with electrically-operated front windows or a central door locking system. Vehicles with a central door locking system also have an additional relay located under the instrument panel.

Where a radio/cassette player is installed, an in-line 2A fuse is located in the power line and is accessible once the dash lower trim panel has been removed.

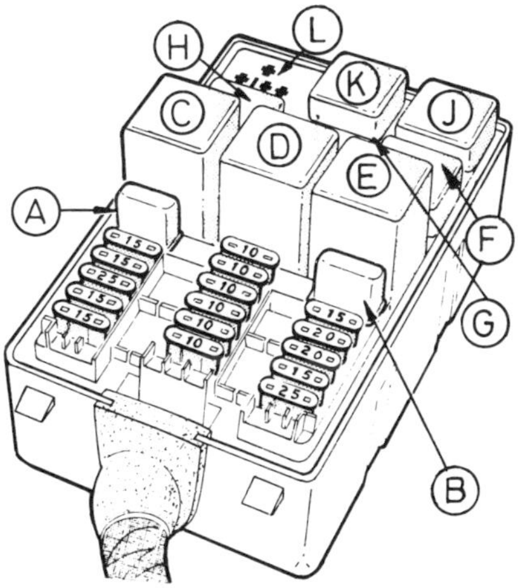

Fuse and relay box

- *A* *Overload circuit breaker (electric windows)*
- *B* *Overload circuit breaker (central door locking)*
- *C* *Wiper delay relay*
- *D* *Headlamp wash relay*
- *E* *Direction indicator relay*
- *F* *Auxiliary driving lamp relay*
- *G* *Spare*
- *H* *Ignition relay*
- *J* *Tailgate heated window relay*
- *K* *Foglamp relay*
- *L* *Spare*

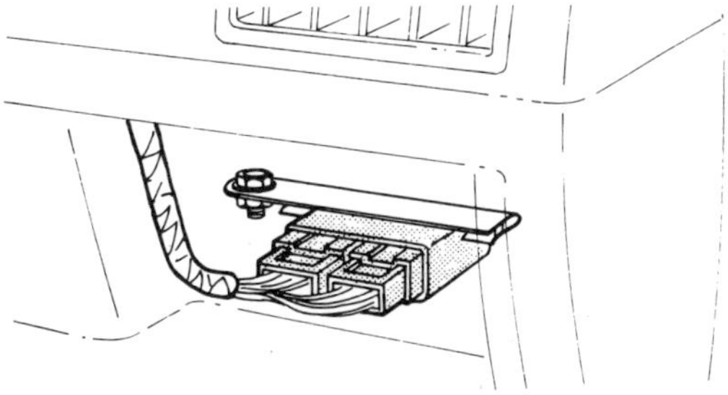

Additional relay under instrument panel on vehicles with central door locking system

Save It!

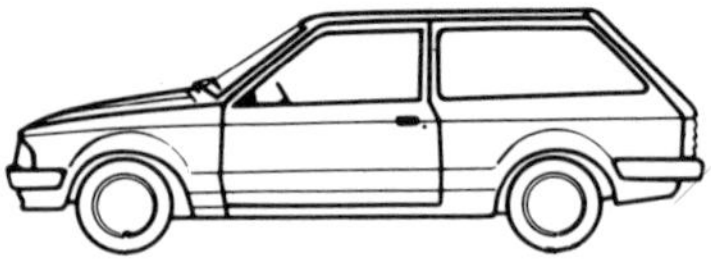

Do-it-yourself car servicing is all about money saving, whilst not forgetting the ever-important point of maintaining the highest standards of safety. In this Chapter we cover several points which should help reduce your motoring costs – or at least prevent them from increasing quite as fast as they otherwise might these days – without reducing your car's safety.

Tyres

Without any doubt whatever, a steel-belted radial ply tyre will give you much better value for money than a textile radial because, although it will cost a bit more to buy, it will last a great deal longer. Remould tyres can give good service, but they have their limitations when used for family motoring; remould radials now have a more reliable reputation than they had when they first appeared on the market, but sometimes give a bit of trouble when trying to balance them. So, what have we learnt so far? Only that in the broadest terms the more you pay for your tyres, the better value for money you'll get.

Regraded tyres are sometimes available (they used to be known as remould quality or RQ); these are tyres which may have the very slightest of defects in the tread pattern or moulding, but are otherwise perfect. If you get the chance to buy these, buy them – to all intents and purposes they're as good as a new tyre.

It's not generally realised that most major tyre manufacturers also produce tyres under a less well known name at a somewhat cheaper price. These are first class buys too – ask any tyre dealer.

Talking of tyre dealers, it's worth mentioning that they're the people to go to if you're intent on saving money (and who isn't these days?). Unless there's a 'special offer' going, the most expensive place to get your tyres will normally be your local garage.

Now let's just briefly consider how to make tyres last. First keep them inflated properly (see *Filling Station Facts* for the correct pressures). Second, drive sensibly (ie no race-track starts or cornering). Third, make sure the wheels are balanced properly (a job for a garage or tyre specialist).

Batteries

Next to tyres, batteries are the most commonly found parts sold by specialists. A top quality battery may cost up to three times the price of the cheapest one that'll fit your car.

Once again, price is related to quality, but isn't necessarily directly proportional. A battery with a twelve month guarantee ought to last that long and a little bit more, but batteries always seem to fail at embarrassing or inconvenient times, so it's worthwhile getting something a little bit better. Many of the accessory shops and tyre dealers sell good quality batteries with two or three year guarantees. Buy one of these – it'll be worthwhile in the long run and still cost quite a bit less than the dearest ones around. And, if you look after it, it'll look after you, too.

Exhaust systems

The average car gets through several exhaust systems in the course of its life, the actual number depending on the sort of journeys for which the car's used (lots of short journeys will mean condensation remaining inside the exhaust system and helping it to rust out more quickly).

The best place to go when your Escort needs a replacement exhaust (or maybe just part of the system) is one of the specialist 'exhaust centres' which have sprung up in recent years. They keep huge stocks to fit most mass-produced cars, and offer free fitting as well as discount prices on the parts themselves. You'll almost certainly show a worthwhile saving compared with getting your Ford dealer to fit the exhaust (which will involve labour charges as well).

If you're planning to keep your car for several years it would certainly be worth thinking about an exhaust system made from stainless steel. It'll normally cost you considerably more than an ordinary mild steel replacement, but on the other hand should last the remainder of the car's life. If you're interested, talk it over with one of the exhaust specialists – they're usually stockists of the stainless steel kind too.

Lubricants and the like

Good cheap engine oils are available, but because it's so difficult to find out which cheap ones *are* good, it's safest to stay clear of them. There are plenty of good multigrade engine oils on the market and quite a few are available at sensible prices from supermarkets and the D-I-Y motoring and accessory shops.

Unless circumstances should force you to, don't buy oil in pint or half-litre cans. This is the most expensive way of buying, particularly if it's from a filling station. The big 5-litre (they used to be one gallon) cans are adequate for most purposes, and contain just about the right amount for an engine oil change; an extra can for topping-up between oil changes will probably be required, particularly if your pride and joy happens to be a bit of an oil burner.

Oil is also available in larger drums (which can be fitted with a tap) sometimes at an even bigger price saving. A telephone call or visit to nearby wholesalers may well prove worthwhile.

Antifreeze is always cheaper if you go to the motoring shops, but bulk buying doesn't normally apply because you never need to buy in any real quantity.

As for greases, brake fluid, etc, you'll save a little at the motoring shops but again you'll never need large quantities – just make sure that you buy something that's good quality.

Additives

Oil and fuel additives have been with us for a long time and no doubt will be around for many years to come. It's pretty unlikely that there are any bad additives around, but there's not a great deal of evidence to suggest that there are many good ones. The major oil manufacturers will tell you that their oils are adequate on their own, in which case you'll only need additives if the oil you're using isn't much good. A fuel additive of the upper cylinder lubrication type is generally accepted as a good thing, one of its main functions being to prevent carbon building up around the piston rings and ring grooves, which means that the piston rings can seal more effectively. The way in which a car is used, whether it is just a runabout which never gets really warm or spends most of its life on long runs, has a far greater influence than additives in determining engine life.

Fuel

Your car's designed to run on four star fuel. If you buy a lower rating fuel your engine performance (and probably your engine too) will suffer. If you *are* forced to buy inferior fuel, drive carefully until you can get the correct grade; in these circumstances it's also beneficial to retard the ignition by a couple of degrees, but you've got the bother of resetting it again later.

Engine tuning and maintenance

The term 'tuning' is much misused; it simply means getting the best performance and economy (sometimes one at the expense of the other) from the standard engine. You'll have a job to improve on the specifications and settings laid down by the manufacturers, so these must be your obvious guidelines.

Tampering with the Escort carburettor is 'out'. The unit is factory calibrated and adjusted during production, and apart from altering the throttle speed (idling speed) screw, nothing else should be touched.

If the engine's not serviced occasionally it will deteriorate over a period and eventually become unreliable. To work efficiently the engine must first of all be in good general condition, and secondly it must be in good tune, which means that the spark plugs, distributor contact points (where applicable), carburettor and valve timing components must be in good condition and correctly adjusted.

When these items are allowed to get out of adjustment, the engine suffers from lack of power and the driver's right foot will invariably try to make up for this loss. Any 'saving' made by ignoring the servicing schedules is then paid for indirectly by more frequent visits to the petrol pumps!

Economy devices

Over the years there have been many economy gadgets produced, all promising instant miracles with the minimum of effort to fit. Sad to relate the vast majority are little more than a gimmick, at best theoretically brilliant but leaving much to be desired when fitted.

If you're thinking of fitting an economy device, it can only be assumed that your car isn't giving you the miles per gallon you originally expected when you bought it. Before you lash out with your hard-earned cash, first check that the engine's in good condition and that the necessary adjustments have been made correctly.

If you've recently had your engine reconditioned and are positive that it's adjusted correctly, and yet you still get poor consumption figures, it may be that the carburettor's badly worn or damaged. Your money would therefore be far better spent on having the existing carburettor checked and reconditioned by a carburettor specialist or Ford dealer, than on a dubious gadget.

The distributor and coil are likely trouble spots for poor economy. To get a complete check and diagnosis, take your car to a tuning specialist who has the necessary knowledge, and perhaps electronic diagnosis equipment, to pinpoint a trouble spot in a relatively short time, and you'll soon recover your outlay in cheaper running costs.

One 'economy device' (to use the term in its widest sense) which *can* repay its cost quite quickly is a vacuum or engine performance gauge, such as the 'Milemiser' from Smiths Industries. This enables a constant check to be kept on the engine's operating range and the idea is to keep the needle in the 'good' sector as much as possible – indicating optimum efficiency and therefore minimum fuel consumption. One of these devices will quickly reveal just how important your own right foot is in the fuel economy game!

Driving habits

With the car in a decent state of tune, there's a lot that you, yourself, can do to improve the car's economy simply by your method of driving. It's very tempting at times to do a 'grand prix' start from the traffic lights or to change down and floor the accelerator just to show yourself that you can do it (nobody else cares anyway)!

The art of economical driving is to use the pedals sensibly. There's no need to race the engine and let the clutch slip violently when starting off; a moderate engine speed, and careful engagement of the clutch, will produce the same result with much greater economy, and only a little more slowly. Once moving, try keeping the throttle pedal in the same position while the car accelerates; you may need to ease it down just a little more but don't press it too hard – there's just no need for it. The little time saved in accelerating will be outweighed by the additional time and cost involved the next time you fill up with petrol.

Changing through the gears should be done in just the same way, using the accelerator pedal with care. When you have to change down, there's no need to rev your engine – this is another fuel waster. Similarly, 'blipping' the throttle pedal while impatiently waiting for the lights to turn green is using unnecessary fuel.

Roof racks

The ever-faithful roof rack has proved a boon to so many motorists, for the extra holiday luggage, but how often do you see cars being driven around with an empty roof rack still attached? Many estimates have been made of the increase in fuel consumption caused by a roof rack, due to wind resistance, and the generally accepted figure is around 10%; with a loaded rack, this figure can be as high as 30%. The moral, then, is obvious, don't use a roof rack unless you have to, and always remove it when it's not in use.

The car itself

It seems almost a foregone conclusion that the smaller engined Escorts will be more economical than the larger, and to a certain extent official fuel consumption figures quoted for the range seem to support this view. However, in practice, whilst it's true that the smaller power units *can* give you more mpg, for a car that's well loaded you're going to need to use the gearbox more. This means higher engine speed and consequently less economy, so never rule out the larger capacity engine versions because you think they will use more fuel. Where you might save a little is on a few replacement parts (where these are related to engine size), and insurance.

If available, and provided your budget permits, try to purchase a five-speed version of the particular Escort you're after. The extra economy and performance of the fifth gear will soon repay the initial extra outlay.

Insurance

Like some of the other things that we've discussed, the service you're going to get from your insurance company will be related to the cost of the cover obtained. A cheap policy's good until you need to make a claim, and then the sort of snags you're going to come across are 'How do I get hold of an assessor to inspect the damage?' or 'How will it affect my No Claim Bonus?'

There are one or two legitimate ways of reducing the policy premium, perhaps by insuring for 'owner driver only', 'two named drivers', or an agreement to pay an agreed amount (excess) of any claim. Many large companies have a discount scheme for their employees if they use the same insurance company; this also applies to bank and Civil Service employees. You may also get a better bargain by insuring through one of the Motoring Associations if you're a member.

What it all adds up to is: (1) Insure well; (2) See what you can get in the way of discounts; and (3) Find out exactly what you're covered for.

Buying spare parts

Apart from the oils and greases which you're going to need, it won't be long before you have to buy a few bits and pieces to keep things running smoothly. Please *do* remember to clean up any parts which are traded-in on an exchange basis (eg brake shoes) and wherever possible, check that any replacement parts look the same as the old one, either by direct comparison, if this can be done, or by reference to any of the illustrations in the appropriate Section of this book.

Spare parts and accessories are available from many sources, but the following should act as a good guide when they're required:

Officially appointed garages

Although Ford dealers should be able to supply just about everything for your car, it's generally true to say that the prices may be higher than you might pay for 'pattern' parts. However, buy only Ford genuine parts if your car is still under warranty.

Other garages

In recent years the big British car manufacturers have introduced a replacement parts scheme whereby they market parts for each others' cars under trade names such as Unipart and Motorcraft. Though you'll pay the same sort of prices for any of these parts ranges, you may well find that you local BL, Talbot or General Motors dealer can supply you with guaranteed parts for your Ford, and that can't be a bad thing.

Accessory shops

These are usually the best places to get items like contact breaker points, oil filters, brake shoes and pads, spark plugs, light bulbs, fanbelts, lubricants, touch-up paints etc – the very things you're going to need for the general servicing of the car. They also sell general accessories and charge lower prices but, what's equally important, they have convenient opening hours and can often be found not too far from home.

Motor factors

Good factors will stock all the more important components of the engine, gearbox, suspension and braking systems, and often provide guaranteed parts on an exchange basis. They're particularly useful to the more advanced do-it-yourself motorist.

Vehicle identification numbers

When obtaining spare parts (and sometimes accessories), the very least you must know is the model and year of manufacture of your car. For many items this is all you need to know, but there will soon come a time when you're asked for the engine number or chassis and model number (which you'd always meant to make a note of, but just hadn't got round to!). Make a note of these now, in your diary or inside the back cover of this book. The numbers you're likely to need are:

The Vehicle Identification Number: located on the plate found under the bonnet above the radiator. The plate also carries information concerning paint colour, final drive ratio etc.

The Engine Number: located in one of the following places, according to engine type:

Front right-hand side of engine block
Front face of cylinder block
Front left-hand side of engine block
Cylinder block above clutch bellhousing

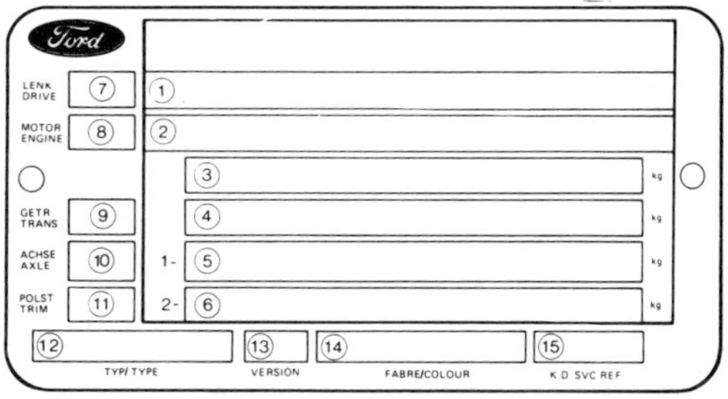

Vehicle identification plate

1 Type approval number
2 Vehicle identification number
3 Gross vehicle weight
4 Gross train weight
5 Permitted front axle loading
6 Permitted rear axle loading
7 Steering (LHD/RHD)
8 Engine
9 Transmission
10 Axle (final drive ratio)
11 Trim (interior)
12 Body type
13 Special territory version
14 Body colour
15 KD reference (usually blank)

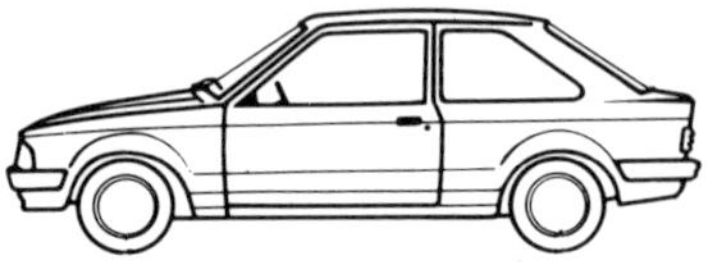

Vital Statistics

You're going to need to know most of the information in this Chapter at some time or other (even if it's only to win a bet in the pub!). Let's go in head first then, starting with the engine ...

ENGINE (OHV)

General specifications	
Engine type	4 cylinder in-line, overhead valve, mounted transversely with transmission at front of vehicle
Capacity	1117 cc
Bore	73.96 mm (2.91 in)
Stroke	64.98 mm (2.56 in)
Compression ratio	9.15 : 1
Output	55 bhp (40 kW) at 5700 rpm
Torque	60 lbf ft (82 Nm) at 4000 rpm
Firing order	1 – 2 – 4 – 3 (No 1 at timing cover end of engine)
Cylinder head	
Material	Cast iron
Valve clearances (cold)	
Inlet	0.22 mm (0.009 in)
Exhaust	0.59 mm (0.023 in)
Lubrication	
Minimum oil pressure at 80°C (175°F):	
Engine speed 750 rpm	0.6 kgf/cm^2 (8.5 lbf/in^2)
Engine speed 2000 rpm	1.5 kgf/cm^2 (21.3 lbf/in^2)
Engine oil capacity:	
Without filter change	2.75 litres (4.8 Imp pints)
With filter change	3.25 litres (5.7 Imp pints)

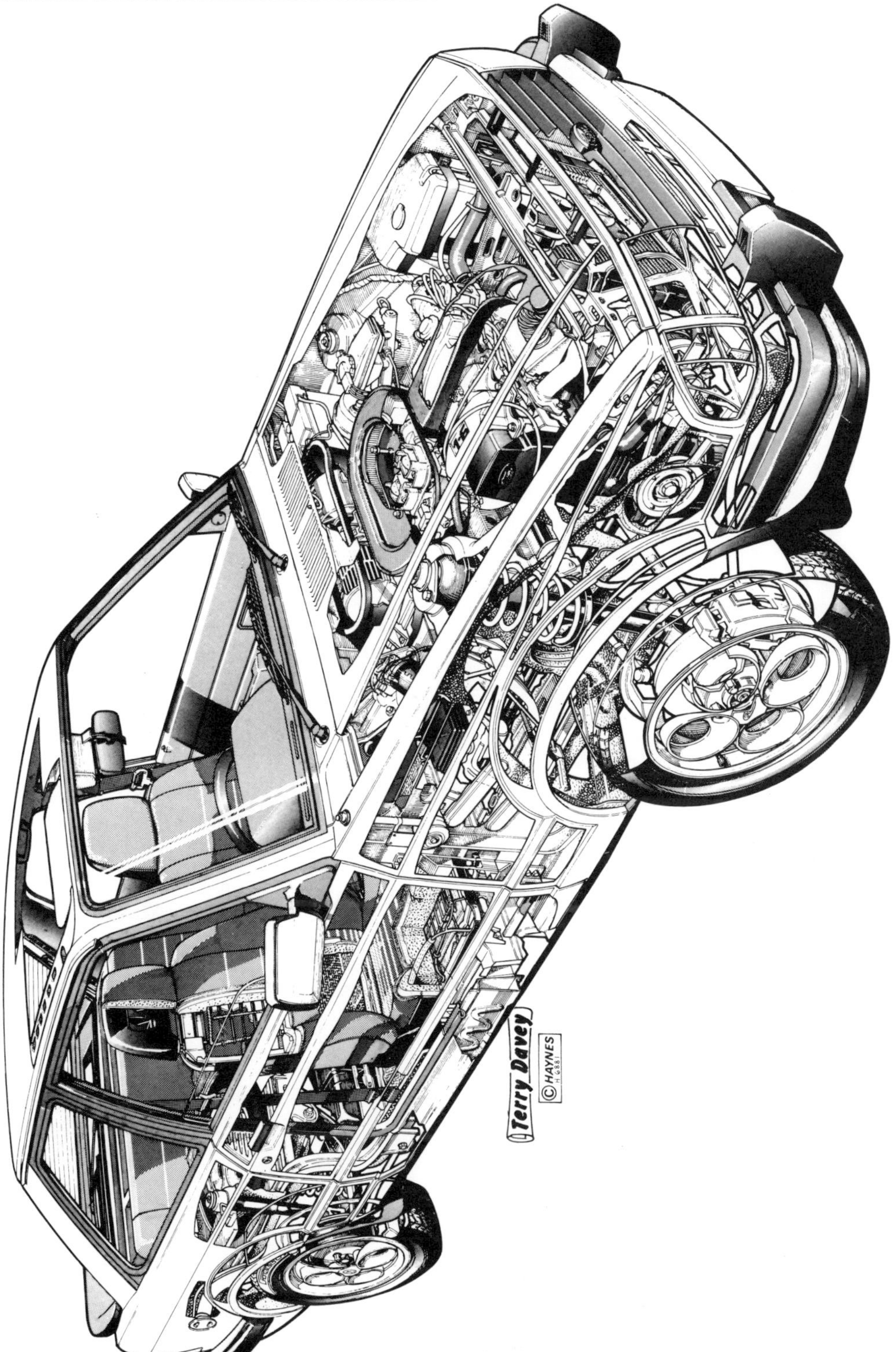
Terry Davey
© HAYNES
H 6881
1.6

ENGINE (CVH)

General specifications

Engine type	4-cylinder, in-line, overhead camshaft, mounted transversely with transmission at front of vehicle
Cubic capacity:	
1.1 litre nominal	1117 cc
1.3 litre nominal	1296 cc
1.6 litre nominal	1597 cc
Bore:	
1.1	73.96 mm (2.91 in)
1.3 and 1.6	79.96 mm (3.15 in)
Stroke:	
1.1	64.98 mm (2.56 in)
1.3	64.52 mm (2.54 in)
1.6	79.52 mm (3.13 in)
Compression ratio	9.5 : 1 (except 1.1 LC 8.5 : 1)
Power output:	
1.1 LC	55 bhp (40 kW) at 6000 rpm
1.1 HC	59 bhp (43 kW) at 6000 rpm
1.3 HC	69 bhp (51 kW) at 6000 rpm
1.6 HC	79 bhp (58 kW) at 5800 rpm
1.6 HC/2V	96 bhp (71 kW) at 6000 rpm
Maximum torque:	
1.1 LC	59 lbf ft (80 Nm) at 4000 rpm
1.1 HC	62 lbf ft (84 Nm) at 4000 rpm
1.3 HC	74 lbf ft (100 Nm) at 3500 rpm
1.6 HC	92 lbf ft (125 Nm) at 3000 rpm
1.6 HC/2V	98 lbf ft (132.5 Nm) at 4000 rpm
Firing order	1 – 3 – 4 – 2 (No 1 at timing belt end)

Cylinder head

Material	Light alloy

Lubrication

Minimum oil pressure at 80°C (176°F):	
At 750 rpm	1.0 kgf/cm^2 (14 lbf/in^2)
At 2000 rpm	2.8 kgf/cm^2 (41 lbf/in^2)
Engine oil capacity:	
Without filter change	3.50 litres (6.2 Imp pints)
With filter change	3.75 litres (6.6 Imp pints) 3¾ LETRES

COOLING SYSTEM

System type	Radiator with expansion tank, belt-driven coolant pump and electric radiator fan. Semi-pressurised system on 1.1 engines; fully pressurised on 1.3 and 1.6 engines
Radiator type	Crossflow, fin on tube
Thermostat	
Type	Wax
Opening temperature	85° to 89°C (185° to 193°F)
Fully open temperature	99° to 102°C (210° to 216°F)
Coolant pump	
Type	Centrifugal with vee belt drive (ohv) or driven from toothed timing belt (CVH)

Drivebelt tension (ohv)	12.5 mm (0.5 in) total deflection at centre of longest run

Pressure cap rating

1.1	0.9 kgf/cm^2 (13 lbf/in^2)
1.3 and 1.6	0.85 kgf/cm^2 (12 lbf/in^2)

Capacity

1.1 ohv	5.3 litres (9.3 pints)
1.1 ohc (small radiator)	6.2 litres (10.9 pints)
1.1 ohc (large radiator)	7.2 litres (12.7 pints)
1.3 ohc	7.1 litres (12.5 pints)
1.6 ohc	6.9 litres (12.1 pints) 3½ LITRES

Antifreeze

Recommended concentration (UK)	45% by volume

FUEL SYSTEM

System type	Rear mounted fuel tank, mechanically-operated fuel pump, thermostatically controlled air cleaner and Ford variable venturi (VV) or Weber dual venturi (2V) carburettor

Fuel tank

Capacity	40 litres (8.8 gallons)

Air cleaner

Element type	Paper, disposable
Heat sensor rating:	
With Ford VV carburettor	20°C (68°F) ± 2°C (3°F)
With Weber 2V carburettor	28°C (82°F) ± 2°C (3°F)

Carburettors

Types:	
Ford variable venturi (VV)	Downdraught with sonic idle circuit, coolant-heated automatic choke and anti-run-on valve (all models except XR3)
Weber dual venturi (2V)	Fixed jet with electrically-heated automatic choke and anti-run-on valve (XR3 models)

Ford carburettor tuning data

Idle speed	750 to 850 rpm (fan in operation)
Idle mixture setting (CO level)	1.0 to 2.0%

Weber carburettor tuning data

Idle speed	775 to 825 rpm (fan in operation)
Idle mixture setting (CO level)	1.0 to 1.50%

IGNITION SYSTEM

Mechanical system (1.1 engines)

General

System type	Battery, coil, distributor with mechanical contact breaker
Polarity	Negative earth

Firing order:	
ohv engines	1-2-4-3 (No 1 at timing cover end)
CVH engines	1-3-4-2 (No 1 at timing belt end)
Ignition timing	12° BTDC at 750 to 850 rpm
Distributor	
Make	Bosch (all engines) or Lucas (CVH only)
Rotation of rotor arm	Anti-clockwise viewed from cap
Contact breaker points gap:	
Bosch distributor	0.4 to 0.5 mm (0.016 to 0.020 in)
Lucas distributor	0.4 to 0.6 mm (0.016 to 0.024 in)
Dwell angle	48° to 52°
Spark plugs	
Type:	
ohv engines	Motorcraft AGRF 22 or equivalent
CVH engines (HC)	Motorcraft Super AGPR 12C, AGP 12C or equivalent
CVH engines (LC)	Motorcraft Super AGP 22C
Electrode gap:	
ohv engines	0.75 mm (0.030 in)
CVH engines	0.60 mm (0.025 in)

Electronic system (1.3 and 1.6 engines)

General	
System type	Battery coil, distributor incorporating electronic module
Polarity	Negative earth
Firing order	1-3-4-2 (No 1 at timing belt end of engine)
Ignition timing	12° BTDC at 800 rpm
Distributor	
Type	Bosch or Lucas breakerless
Rotation direction	Anti-clockwise viewed from cap
Spark plugs	
Type:	
1.3	Motorcraft AGP 22C
1.6 (Weber carburettor)	Motorcraft Super AGP 12C or Super AGPR 12C
1.6 (Ford carburettor)	Motorcraft Super AGPR 12C
Electrode gap	0.60 mm (0.025 in)

CLUTCH

General	
Type	Single dry plate, diaphragm spring
Actuation	Cable with automatic adjuster
Driven plate	
Diameter:	
1.1 Hatchback	165 mm (6.5 in)
1.1 Estate and 1.3 models	190 mm (7.5 in)
1.6 (all models)	200 mm (7.9 in)
Pedal stroke	155 mm (6.1 in)

TRANSMISSION

Transmission type	4 or 5 forward speeds and 1 reverse, synchromesh on all forward gears	
Ratios (:1)	**1.1 and 1.3**	**1.6**
Gear ratios:		
1st	3.58	3.15
2nd	2.05	1.91
3rd	1.35	1.28
4th	0.95	0.95
5th (where applicable)	0.76	0.76
Reverse	3.77 (4-sp),3.62 (5-sp)	3.62
Final drive ratios:		
1.1	4.06	
1.3	3.84	
1.6	3.58	
XR3	3.84	

Lubrication

Lubricant type	SAE 80EP gear oil to Ford spec SQM-2C9008-A
Lubricant capacity	2.8 litres (4.9 pints) – four-speed 3.1 litres (5.5 pints) – five-speed

DRIVESHAFTS

Type

Right-hand	Tubular, three-section with two constant velocity (CV) joints
Left-hand	Solid, three-section with two CV joints

Driveshaft identification marks

1.1 models	Yellow
1.3 and 1.6 models	Blue

BRAKING SYSTEM

System type	Hydraulic, dual circuit, discs front, drums rear. Servo standard or option according to model. Handbrake mechanical to rear wheels only

Disc brakes

Caliper type	Single piston, sliding type
Disc diameter	239.45 mm (9.43 in)
Disc thickness:	
1.1 and 1.3 (solid)	10.0 mm (0.39 in)
1.6 (ventilated)	24.0 mm (0.95 in)
Minimum pad friction material thickness	1.5 mm (0.06 in)

Drum brakes

Drum diameter	180.0 mm (7.2 in)
Minimum shoe friction lining thickness	1.0 mm (0.04 in)

STEERING SYSTEM

Type	Rack-and-pinion with universally jointed steering shaft and deformable column

Turning circle

Between kerbs	10.05 m (32.9 ft)
Between walls	10.56 m (34.6 ft)

VITAL STATISTICS

Front wheel alignment

Tolerance permitted when checking	1.5 mm (0.06 in) toe-in to 5.5 mm (0.22 in) toe-out
Adjust to	1.0 mm (0.04 in) toe-in to 3.0 mm (0.12 in) toe-out

SUSPENSION

Front suspension

Type	Independent, MacPherson strut. 1.1 with tie-rod to lower arm, 1.3 and 1.6 with anti-roll bar

Rear suspension

Type	Independent with coil springs, hydraulic shock absorbers and tie-bars
Toe setting	1.63 mm (0.06 in) toe-out to 3.87 mm (0.15 in) toe-in

Roadwheels and tyres

Wheel sizes:		
Pressed steel (Lo series)	13 x 4.50, 13 x 5.00	
Pressed steel (Hi series)	13 x 5.00	
Cast alloy	14 x 5.50	
Tyre sizes	145 SR 13, 155 SR 13, 175/70 SR 13, 175/70 HR 13 or 185/60 HR 14, depending on model	
Tyre pressures (cold) in bar (lbf/in^2):	**Front**	**Rear**
With up to 3 occupants	1.8 (26)	1.8 (26)
Fully laden	2.0 (28)	2.3 (33)

ELECTRICAL SYSTEM

System type	12V, negative earth with belt-driven alternator and pre-engaged starter motor
Battery	12V Lead/acid, 35 to 50 Ah depending upon vehicle model

Alternator	**Bosch**	**Lucas**	**Motorola**
Rated output (13.5V at 6000 rpm engine speed)	28A (G1-28A)	28A (A115/28)	28A (265 OD)
	35A (K1-35A)	35A (A115/36)	35A (2652 F)
	45A (K1-45A)	45A (A133/45)	45A (2627 G)
	55A (K1-55A)	55A (A133/55)	

Starter motor

Type	Pre-engaged
Make:	
Lucas	8M 90 or 9M 90
Bosch	0.8 kW, 0.85 kW or 0.9 kW
Nippondenso	0.6 kW or 0.9 kW

Bulbs

Headlamp:	
Halogen	60/55W
Tungsten	50/45W
Front parking lamp	4W
Front indicator lamp	21W
Side repeater lamp	5W
Stop/tail lamp	25/5W

Reversing lamp	21W
Rear foglamp	21W
Rear indicator lamp	21W
Rear number plate lamp	5W
Auxiliary lamp (Halogen)	55W
Foglamp (Halogen)	55W
Instrument cluster warning lamps	1.3W
Panel illumination	2.6W
Cigar lighter illumination	1.4W
Glove compartment lamp	2W
Luggage compartment lamp	10W
Interior lamp	10W

Fuse – see **'In an emergency'**

DIMENSIONS AND WEIGHTS

Dimensions

Overall length:	
Hatchback	4059 mm (159.8 in)
Estate	4123 mm (162.3 in)
Overall width:	
Hatchback and Estate	1588 mm (62.5 in)
Overall height:	
Hatchback	1336 mm (52.6 in)
Estate	1341 mm (52.8 in)
Track:	
Front	1390 mm (54.7 in)
Rear	1430 mm (56.3 in)

Weights

Gross vehicle weights:	
1.1 Hatchback	1300 kg (2867 lb)
1.1 Estate	1375 kg (3032 lb)
1.3 and 1.6 Hatchbacks and Estates	1375 kg (3032 lb)
Kerb weights:	
1.1 Hatchback	810 kg (1786 lb)
1.3 and 1.6 Hatchbacks	920 kg (2029 lb)
All Estates	915 kg (2018 lb)
Maximum trailer weight:	
1.1	300 kg (662 lb)
1.3 and 1.6	900 kg (1985 lb)
Roof rack load	75 kg (165 lb) maximum, evenly distributed

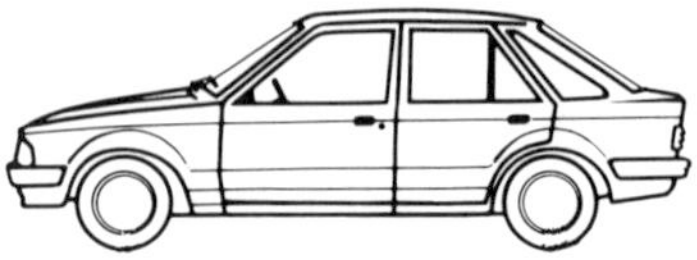

Tools for the Job

For anyone intending to tackle car servicing, a selection of good down-to-earth tools is a basic requirement. The initial outlay, even though it may appear to be something approaching the national defence budget, could well be less than the labour charges for one full service; on top of this, you should be paying less for the oil and replacement parts by getting them yourself, so provided you've two or three hours to spare, you must be on to a winner.

The tools supplied with the vehicle allow you to change a roadwheel and that's about all. The absolute minimum tool kit you'll need to carry out any sort of maintenance and servicing will be a range of metric spanners, two screwdrivers (one for Phillips type screws) and a pair of pliers. With a bit of luck and ingenuity these items should get you through the routine servicing jobs, but they won't do much else.

A small but important point when buying tools is the quality. You don't have to buy the very best in the shop but, on the other hand, the cheapest probably aren't much good. Have a word with the manager or proprietor if you're in doubt; he'll tell you what's good value for money.

It's very difficult to tell you exactly what you're going to need, but the list below should be a great help in building up a good tool kit. Combination spanners (ring one one, open-ended the other) are recommended because, although more expensive than double open-ended ones, they give the advantages of both types.

Combination spanners to cover the range 7 mm to 24 mm
Adjustable spanner – 9 inch
Spark plug spanner (with rubber insert)
Spark plug gap adjustment tool

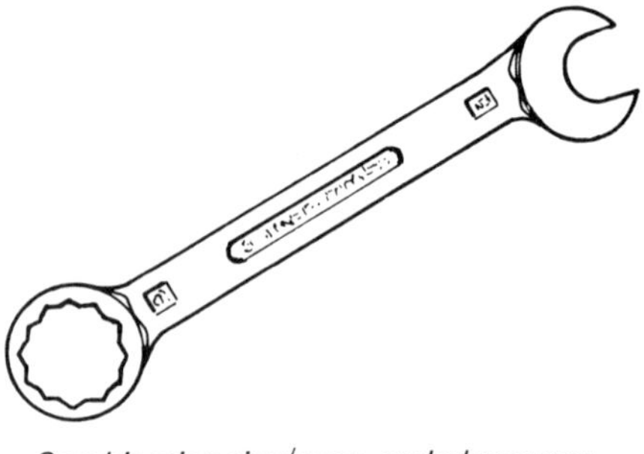

Combination ring/open-ended spanner

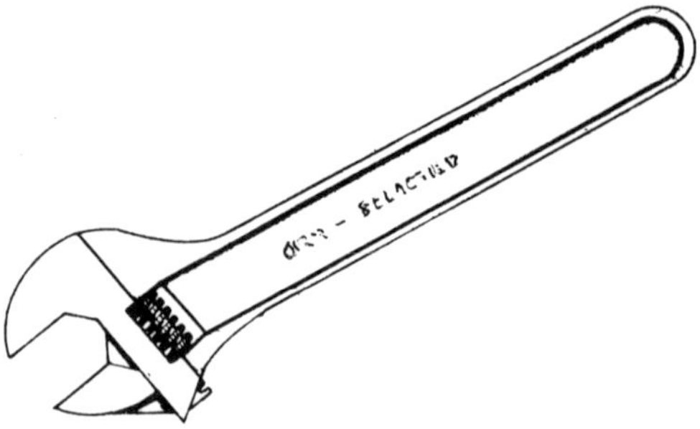

Adjustable spanner

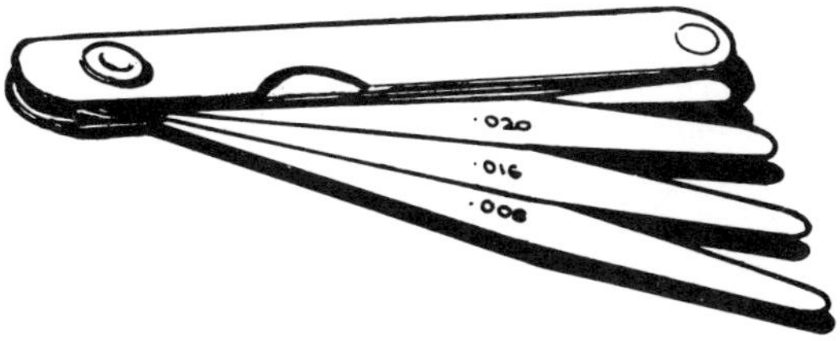

Feeler gauges

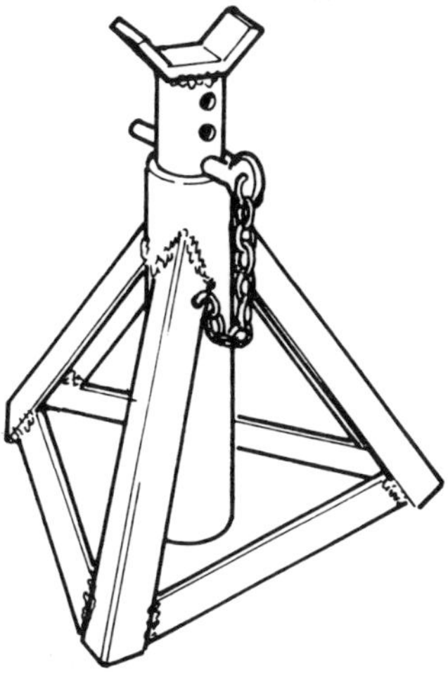

Axle stand

Steel ramp

Set of feeler gauges
Screwdriver – 4 in blade x $\frac{1}{4}$ dia (plain)
Screwdriver – 4 in blade x $\frac{1}{4}$ in dia (crosshead)
Pliers – 6 inch
Junior hacksaw
Tyre pump
Tyre pressure gauge
Oil can
Fine emery cloth or oilstone
Wire brush (small)
Funnel (medium size)
Hydraulic jack or strong scissor type
Pair of stands (concrete or wooden blocks will do if you're careful about choosing them)
Hose brush

You may find that a pair of metal ramps is a very useful investment, providing an alternative to the jack or axle stands when you want to get at the underside of the car but don't need to remove the wheel(s). Most ramps available give a lift of between 9 inches and 1 ft and you can, of course, drive either the front or back end of the car on to them – but you'll still need to apply the handbrake and chock the other wheel(s) for safety's sake.

Hopefully, your attempts at car servicing are going to show you that it can all be worthwhile, and having worked your way through the various jobs listed in the Service Schedules you'll be able to see that there are many others which can be done without becoming a mechanical wizard. For this purpose, Haynes publish a first class Owner's Workshop Manual for the Escort range which details just about every operation that can conceivably be done on these cars. It'll mean buying a few more tools, but you'll save yourself still more money and get a good job done in the process.

While we're talking about tools, it's worth mentioning some of the tune-up aids that are on the market. A visit to a good motor accessory shop can be an enlightening experience, just to show you the sort of things available. Later in this book, you'll find a bit about 'bolt-on goodies', but all we'll concern ourselves with here are three items.

Stroboscopic timing light

The most accurate way of checking ignition timing (that's the time at which the spark occurs) is with the engine running, and for this a stroboscopic (strobe) light us used. This is connected to No. 1 spark plug lead and the beam is shone on to the crankshaft pulley mark. Any proprietary light should come with full connecting and operating instructions.

Dwell meter

This is used for measuring the period of time for which the distributor points remain closed during the ignition cycle, and provides a more accurate method of setting-up the ignition than can be done by simply setting the points gap. Dwell angle meters normally incorporate a tachometer (rev counter if you prefer) which can be useful for checking engine idle speed.

Cylinder compression gauge

This is very useful for tracing the cause of a fall-off in engine performance. It consists of a pressure gauge and non-return valve, and is simply screwed into a spark plug hole while the engine is turned over on the starter, with the throttle held wide open.

Two other useful items are a hydrometer, which is used for checking the specific gravity of the battery electrolyte (this will tell you if you have a dud cell which won't hold a charge), and a 12-volt lamp on an extension lead with crocodile clips which can be connected to the battery terminals.

Care of your tools

Having bought a reasonable set of tools and equipment, it's the easiest thing in the world to abuse them. After use, always wipe off any dirt and grease using a clean, dry cloth before putting them away. Never leave them lying around after they've been used. A simple rack on the garage wall, for things you don't need to carry in the car, is a good idea.

Keep all your spanners and the like in a metal box – you can wrap some rags around them to stop them rattling if you're going to carry them in the boot of the car. Any gauges and meters should be carefully put away so that they don't get damaged or rusty. Do take a little care over maintaining your tools too. Screwdriver blades, for example, inevitably lose their keen edges, and a little timely attention with a file or oilstone won't go amiss.

Service Scene

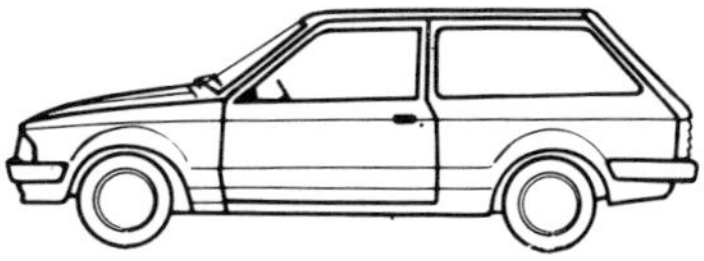

We've now discussed some of the more important features of your car, and also given some thought to equally important things like tools, money saving and so on. Now to the nitty-gritty of servicing – perhaps the very thing you've dreaded for so long? It's not as difficult as you think ...

The Ford models are an up-to-date design which, if it means nothing more to you, does offer the advantage of fairly widely spaced service intervals and a general reduction in the number of items requiring attention. This has developed from the increased use of sealed-for-life bearings, nylon bushes, better metal and lubricant technology, and a reduction in the number of moving parts (which tends to make some people think the car will go on forever without any regular attention because half the bits don't exist anymore!).

It's still important to carry out servicing and inspection at regular intervals to keep the car safe, to prolong its active life, and to maintain a sensible resale value. The old maxim of prevention rather than cure was never truer than in connection with car servicing. Whether it be casting your eagle eye over the general workings of the car or getting down to the service task in a workmanlike (or workwomanlike) fashion, it's all going to be worthwhile in the long run. Remember that a worn part won't put itself right and isn't a thing to be lived with. Fix it as soon as you find it, even if it's not time for the next service.

In this Chapter, we've tried to present the servicing tasks in a logical way to minimize the amount of jacking up etc, which may be a prelude to the actual job. The items are basically those recommended by the car manufacturers, but are supplemented by some additional ones which we think are well worth the extra trouble.

If you've recently bought the car, the safest thing is to go right through all the Service Schedules (not on the same day, of course!) unless you can really satisfy yourself that the previous owner was as meticulous about things as you'd like to be. You'll see that we've included Spring and Autumn check-ups too, just so you can make sure your car's as fit as possible for the season ahead.

Asbestos

Certain friction, insulating, sealing, and other products – such as brake linings, brake bands, clutch linings, torque converters, gaskets, etc – contain asbestos. *Extreme care must be taken to avoid inhalation of dust from such products since it is hazardous to health.* If in doubt, assume that they *do* contain asbestos.

Safety

Accidents do happen, but 99% of them can be prevented by taking a little care. We're going to list a few points which should reduce any accident risk, and we'd like you to read through them before starting work – it could prove to be very worthwhile.

DO wipe up grease or oil from the floor if you spill any (and you will do, sooner or later).

DO get someone to check regularly that everything's OK if you're likely to be spending some time underneath the car.

DON'T use a file or similar tool without a handle. The tang can give you a nasty gash if something goes wrong.

DO make sure when you're using a spanner, that it's the right size for the nut and that it's properly fitted before tightening or loosening.

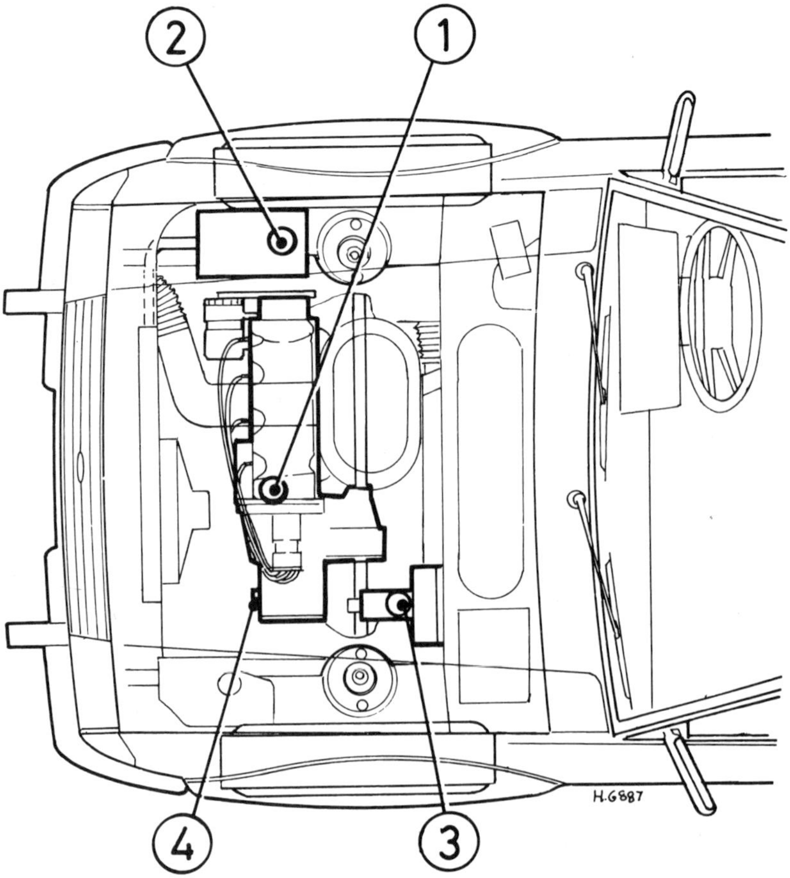

Lubricants and fluids

Component or system	Lubricant/fluid type or specification	Castrol product
1 Engine	*Multigrade engine oil SAE 10W/30*	*GTX*
2 Cooling system	*Antifreeze mixture to Ford spec SSM-97B-9103-A*	*Anti-freeze*
3 Brake hydraulic fluid reservoir	*Hydraulic fluid to Ford spec SAM-6C 9101-A/-C, or ESEAM-6C 1001-A*	*Universal Brake and Clutch Fluid*
4 Transmission	*Hypoid gear oil SAE 80EP*	*Hypoy Light*

DO brush away any drilling swarf with an old paintbrush – never with your fingers.

DON'T allow battery acid or battery terminal corrosion to contact the skin or clothes. If it should happen, wash off immediately with plenty of cold running water.

DON'T rush any job – that's how mistakes are made. If you don't think you'll finish the job in time, do it tomorrow, but try not to make this an excuse for forgetting about it.

DO take care when pouring brake fluid. If it spills on the paintwork and isn't removed immediately, it'll take the paint off. And wash your hands well afterwards as it's poisonous.

DON'T run the engine in the garage with the doors closed.

DON'T work in an inspection pit with the engine running – the fumes will tend to concentrate at the lowest point.

DO keep long hair, sleeves, ties and the like well clear of any rotating parts when the engine's running.

DON'T grab hold of ignition HT leads when the engine's running – there's just the possibility of an electric shock, particularly if the leads are dirty or wet.

DO chock the rear wheels when jacking up the front of the car, and vice versa. Where possible, also apply the handbrake and engage first or reverse gear.

DON'T rely on the car jack when you're working underneath. Axle stands, or wooden or concrete blocks should be used, but choose the points of support sensibly to prevent damaging anything.

SERVICE SCHEDULES

WEEKLY, BEFORE A LONG JOURNEY, OR EVERY 250 MILES (400 KM)

The following items are likely to be required:

Antifreeze, engine oil, distilled water, brake fluid, clean tap water, windscreen washer solvent.

1 Check engine oil level

Refer to *Filling Station Facts* for details on how this should be carried out.

2 Check coolant level

Again, reference to *Filling Station Facts* should tell you all you need to know.

3 Tyre pressures and tread wear

And yet again, refer to *Filling Station Facts.*

4 Check battery electrolyte level

The battery's located under the bonnet, at the rear, on the left-hand side. First wipe away any dirt or moisture from the top of the battery so that none can get inside. Remove the caps or cover from the battery cells, and check the electrolyte level (with some types of battery you can see the fluid level through the battery case).

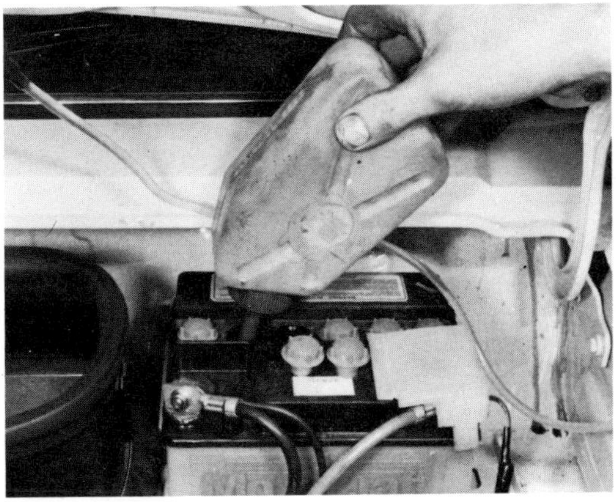

Topping up battery

With an alternator and integral regulator, the addition of water to a battery will be required very rarely. Indeed, frequent topping up indicates that the battery is being overcharged due to a fault in the circuit. Where necessary add distilled water or purified water to bring the electrolyte level just above the tops of the battery plates. With some batteries, distilled water is added to the trough until all the rectangular filling slots are full and the bottom of the trough's just covered.

If for some reason you have no distilled water you can use the frost which collects on the walls of the freezer or fridge, and allow this to melt; if you're really desperate, and as a last resort only, boil up some tap water in the kettle then allow it to cool, but don't make a habit of using this or the battery will suffer in the long run.

Refit the cell caps or cover, carefully wiping up any drops of water that were spilt, then check that the terminals are tight. A very light smear of petroleum jelly can be applied to these to help prevent any corrosion. If the weather's extremely cold, run the engine for a few minutes; this will charge the battery and mix the electrolyte which will prevent the added water from freezing.

Never bring naked lights or flames near the battery even with the vent caps or covers in position, as any escaping hydrogen gas can be explosive!

Never place tools or spanners on top of the battery. They may short circuit the terminals, which is damaging to the cells and will shorten the life of the unit. Keep the terminal screws tight.

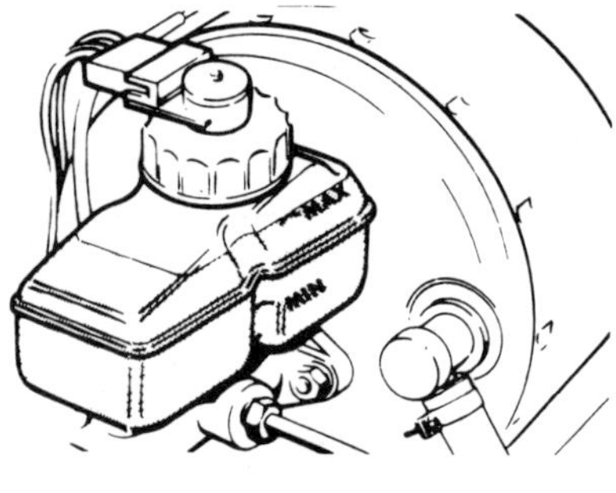

Brake master cylinder fluid reservoir

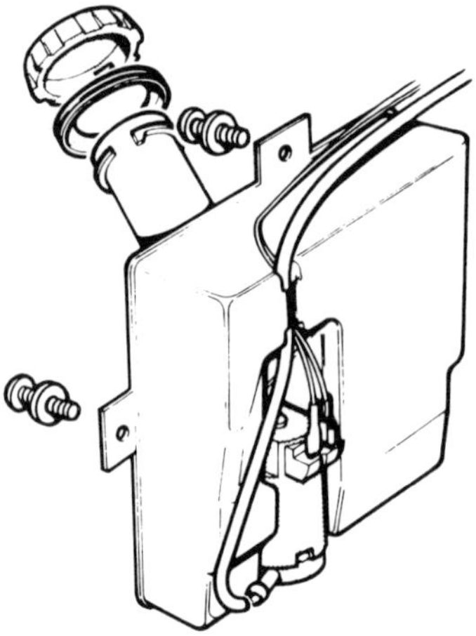

Tailgate washer fluid and pump (car)

Topping up washer fluid reservoir

5 *Check brake master cylinder fluid reservoir*

This is a job that can be done by giving the translucent reservoir a quick glance. The fluid level will only require topping up at very infrequent intervals and any slight drop in level should then only be due to wear in the front disc pads. Wear causes the pads to move nearer to the disc and, as the caliper piston moves out to compensate, the effective volume of the hydraulic system is increased. The level of the fluid should not be allowed to drop below the 'MIN' line. There's a warning light system fitted to the reservoir that will illuminate the warning light on the dashboard should the fluid fall below this level. However, this shouldn't be used as a reason to avoid that quick visual check of the reservoir itself. If you find that the fluid level drops rapidly and frequent topping up is required, then fluid loss is occurring somewhere in the system, and the cause should be investigated immediately.

Only add fluid which has been stored in an airtight container and has remained unshaken for the previous 24 hours. All top quality hydraulic brake fluids are inter-mixable. *Never* use any other type of fluid or oil in the brake hydraulic system. The brake fluid warning light circuit should be checked by turning the ignition key to position II and, with an assistant depressing the centre of the fluid reservoir cap, checking that the dashboard warning lamp is illuminated.

6 *Top up windscreen washer fluid reservoir (and rear window washer fluid reservoir if fitted)*

Pull the cap from the washer reservoir and top up as necessary with clean water. The addition of a good quality solvent will keep the glass free from smears and also prevent the washer fluid freezing in winter. Preferably add the solvent to the water after the reservoir has been filled, as many products tend to foam if they're put in first and then the water poured in. *Never use cooling system antifreeze in the washer reservoir as it will remove the paint from the car bodywork.*

The windscreen washer reservoir is situated on the left-hand side of the engine compartment. The rear screen washer reservoir (where fitted) is situated at the side of the load compartment.

On models equipped with a headlamp washer system, the fluid reservoir is located adjacent to the reservoir for the windscreen washer.

7 *Check condition of windscreen wiper blades*

With time, wiper blades deteriorate. They're affected by oil and fumes which collect on the windscreen, and the wiping action deteriorates. Renewal is the only answer when this occurs, and it's a straightforward operation.

Pull the wiper arm away from the glass until the arm locks. Depress the small clip on the blade and slade the blade out of the hooked part of the arm. Using the thumb, draw back the rubber insert until the spring clip can be removed. Slide the rubber insert from the blade. Refit by reversing the removal operations.

If the wiper arm has to be removed, first apply masking tape alongside the upper edge of the wiper blade onto the windscreen glass as a guide to wiper arm alignment at refitting. Pull the wiper arm away from the screen until it locks. Raise the plastic nut cover, unscrew the nut that holds the wiper arm to the spindle and pull the arm from the spindle splines. Refitting is a reversal of removal, but set the arms in alignment with the masking tape and make sure that the wiper motor was switched off by the wiper switch (not the ignition key) and is in the 'parked' position.

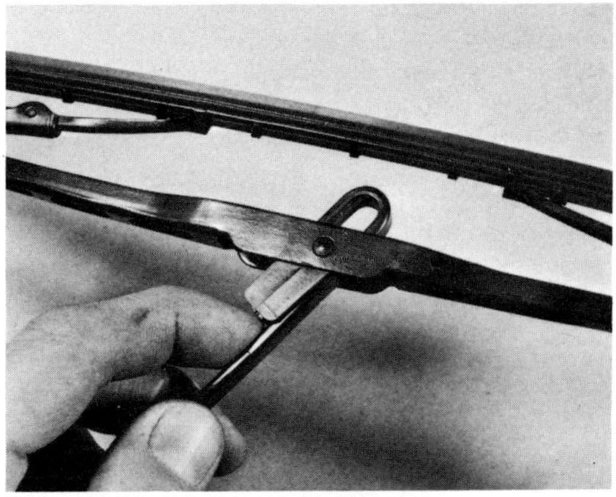

Disconnecting wiper blade from arm

8 Check that all lights work

Switch on the car lights and check that they're all working correctly. Don't forget to include the direction indicators and brake lights, either by getting someone to watch while you operate them or by looking for the tell-tale reflection on the garage wall or adjacent car. (Shop windows can provide a useful check on brake lights – try it next time you're parking in the High Street). If any bulb needs renewing, you'll find the secret of how to get at it revealed in *In an Emergency.* And while you're checking the lights, it makes sense to see that the lenses are clean, front and rear.

9 Relax

That's the first of the regular Service Schedules successfully completed!

Unscrewing wiper arm nut

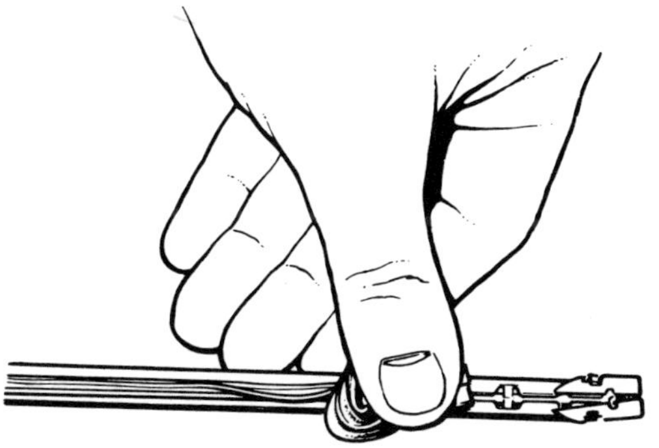

Pushing back wiper blade rubber

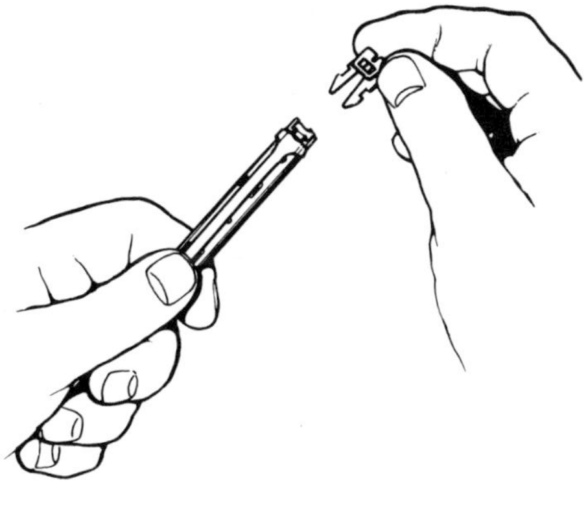

Refitting wiper blade rubber insert clip

AT THE END OF THE FIRST 1500 MILES (2500 KM) – NEW VEHICLES

This schedule should normally be carried out by your dealer as part of the warranty requirement, and is provided here for information only

1 Check the drivebelt tension

A conventional vee drivebelt is used to drive the alternator and coolant pump pulleys on ohv engines, and the alternator pulley on CVH engines, power being transmitted from a pulley on the front end of the crankshaft.

Check that the total deflection of the belt is 0.5 in (12.5 mm) at the mid-point of the longest run of the belt. Grip the belt between finger and thumb for this test.

Where re-tensioning is required, slacken the alternator mounting bolts and the bolts on the adjuster link. Pull the alternator away from the engine until the belt is fairly taut and tighten the adjuster strap bolt. A little trial and error may be required to obtain the correct tension. If the belt is too slack, it will slip and soon become glazed or burnt and the coolant pump (ohv) and alternator will not perform correctly, with consequent overheating of the engine and low battery charge. If the belt is too tight, the bearings in the alternator and/or coolant pump will soon be damaged. Do not lever against the body of the alternator to tension the belt or damage may occur.

2 Check the tightness of the inlet and exhaust manifold bolts

This should be done when the engine is cold. For those who possess a torque wrench, the correct torque wrench settings are:

Ohv engine	
Inlet –	*14 lbf ft (19 Nm)*
Exhaust –	*12 lbf ft (16 Nm)*
CVH engine	
Inlet –	*13 lbf ft (18 Nm)*
Exhaust –	*12 lbf ft (16 Nm)*

3 Check the valve clearances

Only if yours is an ohv type engine – CVH engines have self-adjusting hydraulic tappets

This operation should be carried out with the engine cold and the air cleaner and rocker cover removed.

Using a ring spanner or socket on the crankshaft pulley bolt, turn the crankshaft in a clockwise direction until No 1 piston is at TDC on its compression stroke. This can be verified by checking that the pulley and timing cover marks are in alignment and that the valves of No 4 cylinder are rocking. When the valves

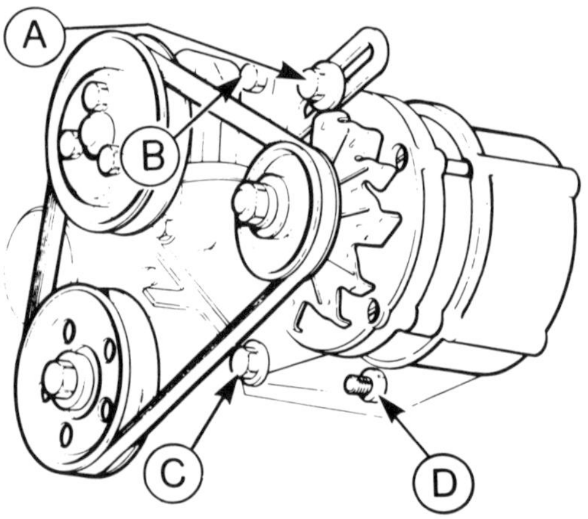

Alternator adjuster and mounting bolts (ohv engine)

A Adjuster link clamp bolt
B Adjuster link-to-block bolt
C Lower front mounting bolt
D Lower rear mounting bolt

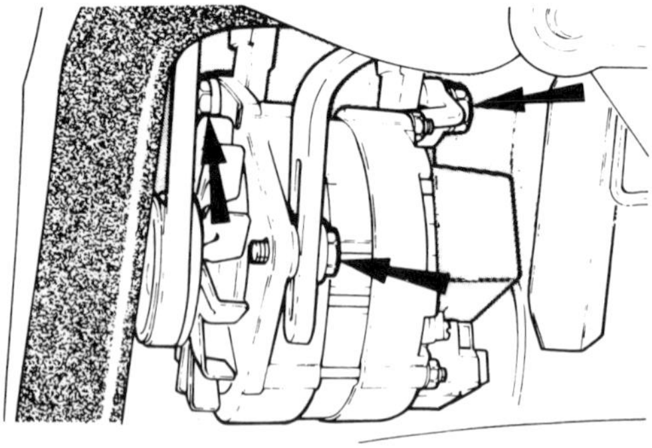

Alternator and adjuster link bolts (CVH engines)

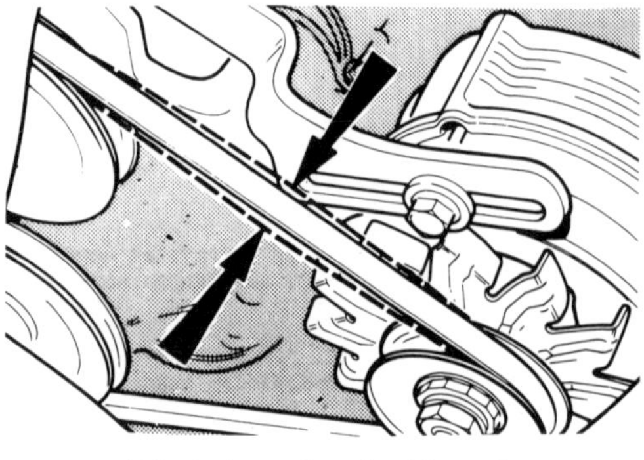

Drivebelt tension checking points

are rocking, this means that the slightest rotation of the crankshaft pulley in either direction will cause one rocker arm to move up and the other to move down.

Numbering from the thermostat housing end of the cylinder head, the valves are identified as follows:

Valve No	**Cylinder No**
1 – Exhaust	*1*
2 – Inlet	*1*
3 – Exhaust	*2*
4 – Inlet	*2*
5 – Exhaust	*3*
6 – Inlet	*3*
7 – Exhaust	*4*
8 – Inlet	*4*

Adjust the valve clearances by following the sequence given in the following table. Turn the crankshaft pulley 180° (half a turn) after adjusting each pair:

Valves rocking	**Valves to adjust**
7 and 8	*1 (Exhaust), 2 (Inlet)*
5 and 6	*3 (Exhaust), 4 (Inlet)*
1 and 2	*7 (Exhaust), 8 (Inlet)*
3 and 4	*5 (Exhaust), 6 (Inlet)*

The clearances for the inlet and exhaust valves are different (see *'Vital Statistics'*). Use a feeler gauge of the appropriate thickness to check each clearance between the end of the valve stem and the rocker arm. The gauge should be a stiff sliding fit. If it is not, turn the adjuster bolt with a ring spanner. These bolts are of stiff thread type and require no locking nut. Turn the bolt clockwise to reduce the clearance and anti-clockwise to increase it.

Refit the air cleaner and rocker cover on completion of adjustment. Check that the rocker cover gasket is in good condition, otherwise renew it.

4 Check the brake hydraulic system unions for leaks

If leaks are evident, check that the unions are tight, otherwise have your dealer rectify the problem.

5 Check engine idle speed

Unless your car is equipped with a tachometer or you can connect a separate instrument, the specified idle speed (see *'Vital Statistics'*) is difficult to estimate.

Make sure that the engine is at normal operating temperature before adjusting (see accompanying illustrations). If you have reason to believe that the mixture setting (tamperproof screw) or the automatic choke adjustment are incorrect, leave any adjustment to your dealer.

6 Check for fluid leaks

The engine compartment should be checked

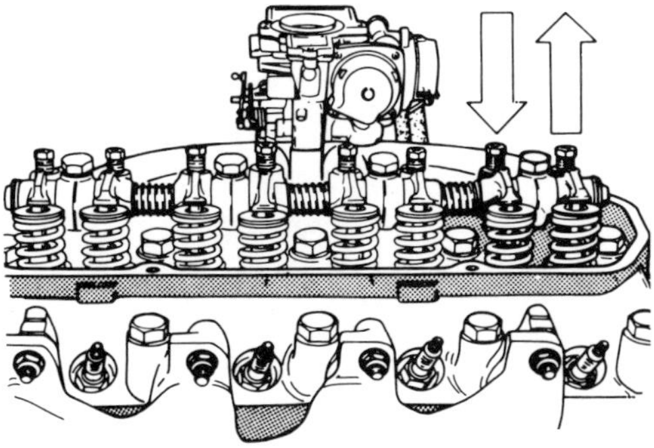

Valves rocking, indicated by movement of rocker arms (arrowed)

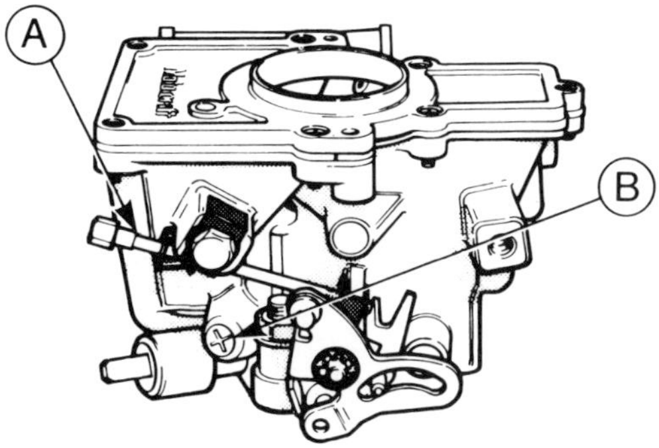

Adjustment screws (Ford VV carburettor)

A Idle speed screw
B Mixture screw (tamperproof cap)

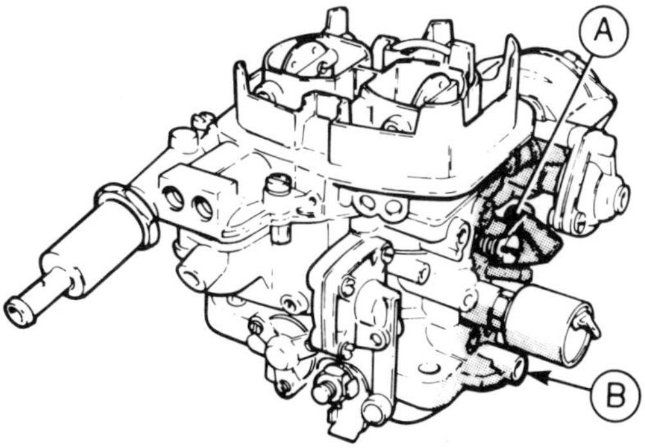

Adjustment screws (Weber 2V carburettor)

A Idle speed screw
B Mixture screw (with tamperproof plug)

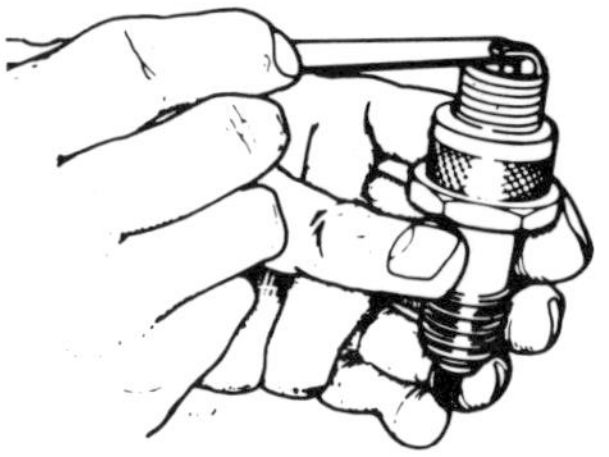

Checking plug gap with feeler gauges

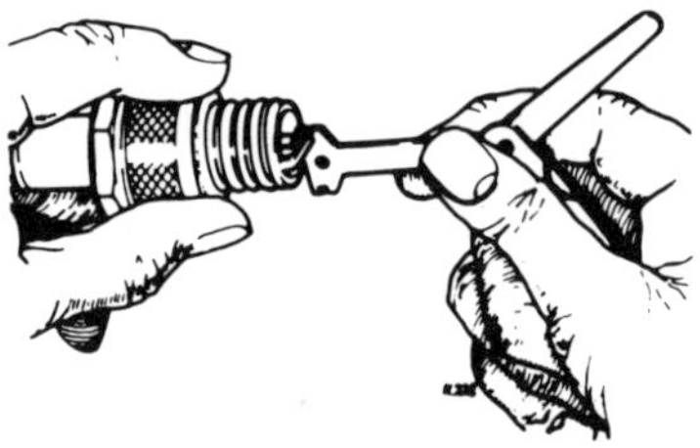

Altering the plug gap. Note use of correct tool

Spark plug maintenance

White deposits and damaged porcelain insulation indicating overheating

Broken porcelain insulation due to bent central electrode

Electrodes burnt away due to wrong heat value or chronic pre-ignition (pinking)

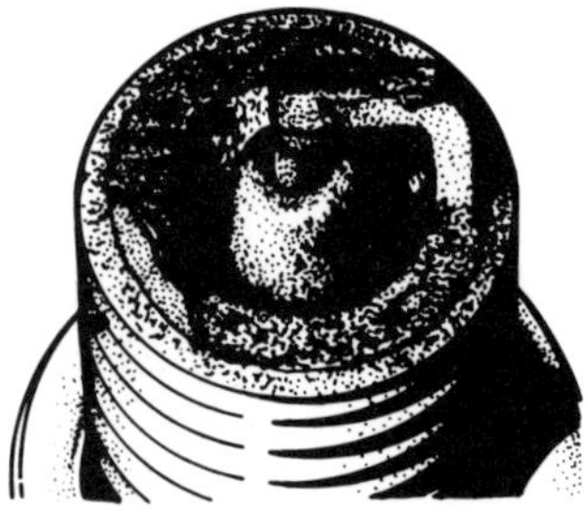

Excessive black deposits caused by over-rich mixture or wrong heat value

Mild white deposits and electrode burnt indicating too weak a fuel mixture

Plug in sound condition with light greyish brown deposits

Spark plug electrode conditions

visually to see that there are no signs of fluid leakage from the engine, ancillary components or connecting hoses. If any are found, their source should be determined and the problem rectified by your dealer.

It is also advisable to check the underside of the car for any possible fluid leakage or damage to fuel or brake lines, etc.

EVERY 6000 MILES (10 000 KM)

(In addition to the items specified in the weekly schedule)

The following items may be required:

Paraffin, oil filter, engine oil, front disc pads, rear brake shoes, alternator drivebelt.

1 Clean and regap the spark plugs

Ohv engines

Before unscrewing the plugs, pull off the leads and brush out any grit from the plug recesses to avoid it dropping into the cylinders as the spark plugs are unscrewed.

The appearance of a removed spark plug can give some indication of the condition or state of tune of the engine, but as modern engines run on a weaker fuel/air mixture in order to conform to current emission control regulations, a rather whiter appearance of the spark plug electrode area must be expected than was the case on older cars. As the mixture control is preset during production, a black appearance of the plug electrode will normally be due to oil passing worn piston rings or valve stem oil seals, unless the carburettor has been tampered with.

Cleaning the electrodes with a wire brush may leave conductance paths so an abrasive type cleaning device is to be preferred, but wash the plugs thoroughly in petrol to remove any abrasive powder, particularly from the threads if they were oily.

Always bend the outer electrode with a proper spark plug gapping tool to set the gaps to the specified clearance (see *'Vital Statistics'*).

When installing the plugs use a long reach socket, apply a little grease to the threads of the plugs, and do not overtighten. Overtightening may damage the plug or its seat.

Periodically wipe over the HT leads with a fuel-moistened cloth. Only pull the leads off by their rubber connectors.

The sockets on the distributor cap should be cleaned if they appear corroded when a lead is detached. A smear of petroleum jelly *(not grease)* applied to the ferrule on the end of the HT lead will help to prevent corrosion.

Never cut a carbon cored type of HT lead in order to insert a radio suppressor. Apart from it being unnecessary, the cable will be ruined.

Examine the inside of the distributor cap. If the contacts are corroded or are excessively burnt, or if the carbon centre contact is worn away, renew the cap. Make sure that the leads are installed in their correct firing order.

CVH engines

In general, the same remarks apply as were made for the ohv engine. Note, however, that a different type of plug is used, and that its electrode gap is different.

Only remove plugs from the ovh engine when it is warm or cold – never when it is hot.

Note that the firing order on the CVH engine is different from the ohv engine.

2 Clean the oil filler cap breather (ohv only)

Disconnect the small hoses from the engine oil

Connecting an HT lead

Typical CVH engine spark plug

filler cap then remove the cap.

Clean the cap thoroughly in paraffin, dry and refit.

3 Adjust contact breaker points dwell angle (mechanical type contact breaker system only)

The dwell angle is the number of degrees through which the distributor cam turns during the period between the instants of closure and opening of the contact breaker points. Checking the dwell angle not only gives a more accurate setting of the contact breaker gap, but this method also evens out any variations in the gap which could be caused by pitting of the points, wear in the distributor shaft or its bushes, or difference in height of any of the cam peaks.

The dwell angle should be checked with a dwell meter connected in accordance with the maker's instructions. Refer to *'Vital Statistics'* for the correct dwell angle. If the dwell angle is too large, increase the points gap. If it is too small, reduce the gap. Details for adjustment of the gap are given in the 12 000 mile service schedule under the sub-section dealing with points renewal.

The dwell angle should always be adjusted before checking and adjusting the ignition timing (see next sub-section).

4 Check ignition timing (mechanical contact breaker system only)

This will be required whenever one of the following operations has been carried out:

(a) Contact breaker points adjusted or renewed
(b) Distributor removed and refitted
(c) Change of fuel octane rating

Before checking the timing, check and adjust the dwell angle as described previously, with the engine at normal operating temperature.

Increase the contrast of the notch in the crankshaft pulley and the appropriate mark on the timing index (see *'Vital Statistics')* by applying quick-drying white paint.

Connect a timing light (stroboscope) in accordance with the manufacturer's instructions. Start the engine and allow it to idle at the specified speed. Disconnect the vacuum pipe from the distributor and plug the pipe with a piece of rod.

If the timing light is now directed at the engine timing marks, the pulley notch will appear to be stationary and opposite the specified mark on the scale. If the marks are not in alignment, release the distributor clamp pinch-bolt (ohv engines) or securing bolts (CVH engines) and turn the distributor in whichever direction is necessary to align the marks.

Retighten the pinch-bolt or securing bolts, switch off the engine, remove the timing light and reconnect the vacuum pipe.

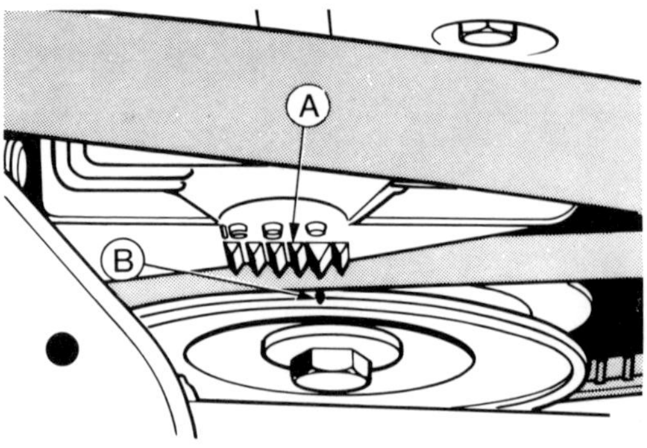

Ignition timing marks (CVH engines)
A Timing cover scale
B Crankshaft pulley notch

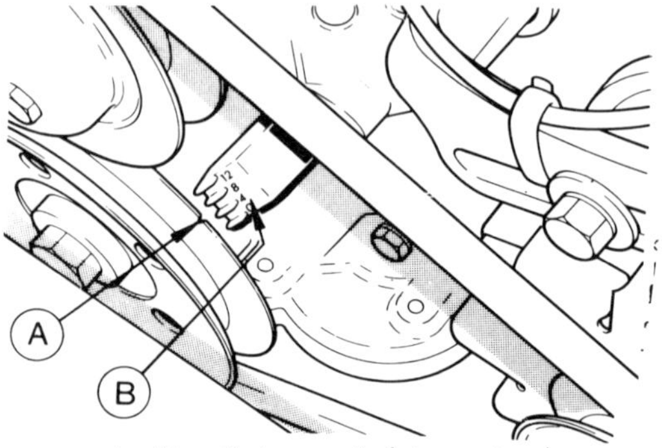

Ignition timing marks (ohv engines)
A Crankshaft pulley notch
B Timing cover scale

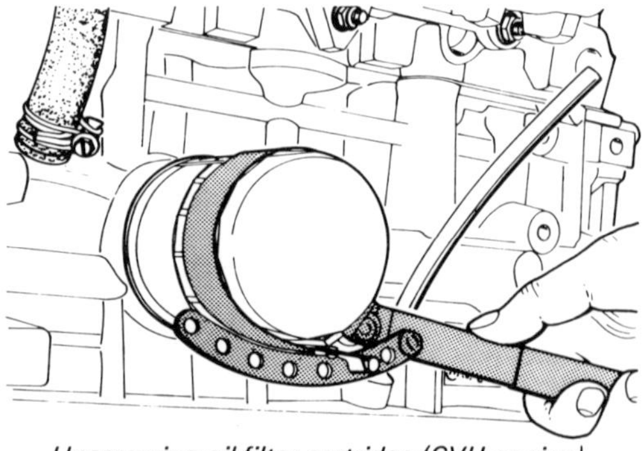

Unscrewing oil filter cartridge (CVH engine)

It may now be necessary to check and adjust the engine idle speed if the distributor setting has to be varied to any extent.

5 Renew the engine oil and filter

It is always best to drain the oil when the engine is hot. Place a bowl or other large container under the engine sump and unscrew the oil filler cap. Unscrew the sump drain plug and wait a few minutes for the oil to drain out completely. Refit the plug and tighten.

The disposable-type cartridge oil filter should now be unscrewed from the side of the crankcase. Several different kinds of wrenches are available for making the job of unscrewing the filter easier, or a small chain wrench can be used. In the absence of a special tool, drive a large screwdriver through the casing of the oil filter and use it as a lever to unscrew the filter.

Wipe the oil filter mounting flange clean and smear some grease onto the filter sealing gasket. Then screw on the new filter as tightly as possible *using hand pressure only, not a tool.*

Fill the engine with the correct grade and quantity of fresh engine oil – see *'Vital Statistics'* and *'Lubrication Chart'*. When the engine is first started after an engine oil change, the oil pressure warning lamp will take a few seconds to go out while the new filter fills with oil – this is normal.

6 Check wear in disc brake pads

Place a mirror between the roadwheel and the caliper and check the thickness of the friction material of the disc pads. If the material has worn down to 1.5 mm (0.060 in) or less, the pads must be renewed as an axle set (four pads).

To renew the pads, slacken the roadwheel bolts, raise the front of the vehicle and remove the roadwheels. Remove the pad retaining clip. Using a 7 mm Allen key, unscrew the bolts until they can be withdrawn from the caliper anchor brackets.

Withdraw the piston housing and tie it up with a length of wire to prevent strain on the flexible hose. Withdraw the inboard pad from the piston housing, then the outboard pad from the anchor bracket.

Clean away all residual dust or dirt, taking care not to inhale the dust as, being asbestos based, it is injurious to health.

Using a piece of flat wood, a tyre lever or similar, push the piston squarely into its bore. This is necessary in order to accommodate the new thicker pads when they are fitted. Depressing the piston will cause the fluid level in the master cylinder reservoir to rise, so anticipate this by syphoning out some fluid using an old hydrometer or poultry baster. Take care not to drip hydraulic fluid onto the paintwork; it acts as an effective paint stripper!.

Commence reassembly by fitting the inboard pad into the piston housing. Make sure that the spring on the back of the pad fits into the piston. Fit the outboard pad into the anchor bracket. Locate the piston housing and screw in the Allen bolts tightly. Fit the retaining clip.

Repeat the operations on the opposite brake.

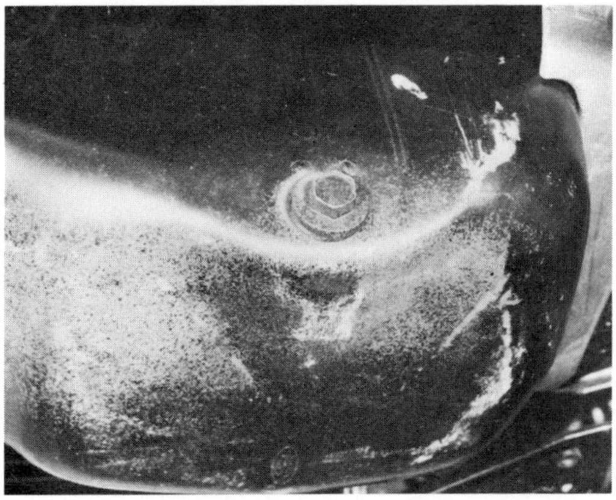

Engine sump drain plug

Screwing on an oil filter cartridge

Disc pad retaining clip

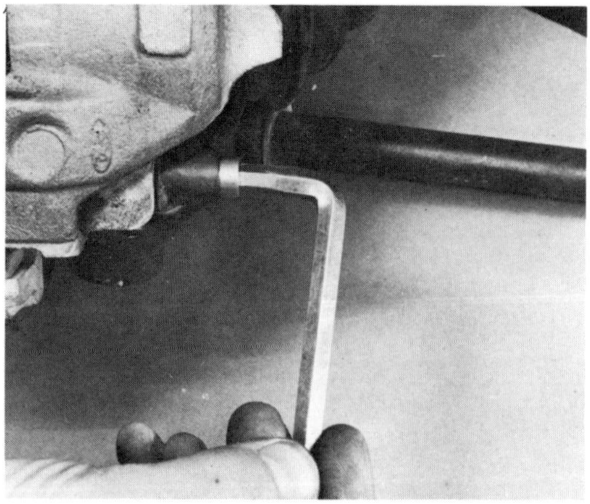

Unscrewing caliper bolt

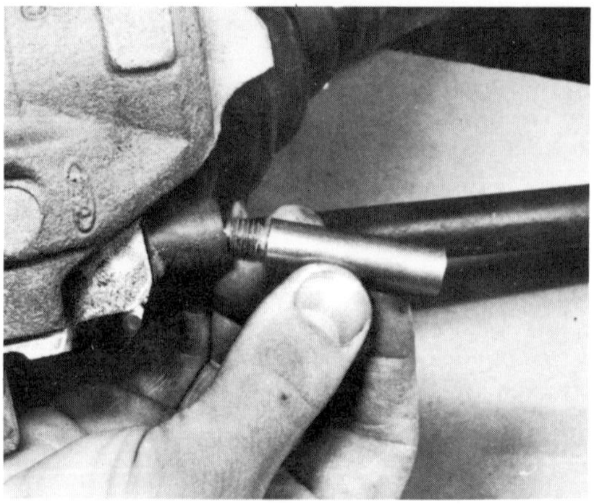

Removing bolt from caliper anchor bracket

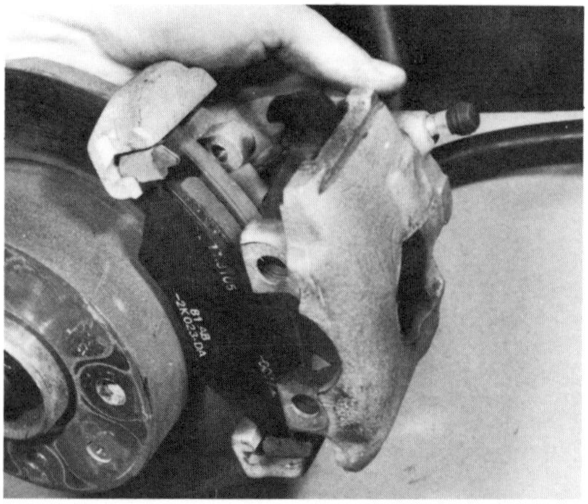

Withdrawing caliper piston housing

Removing inboard disc pad

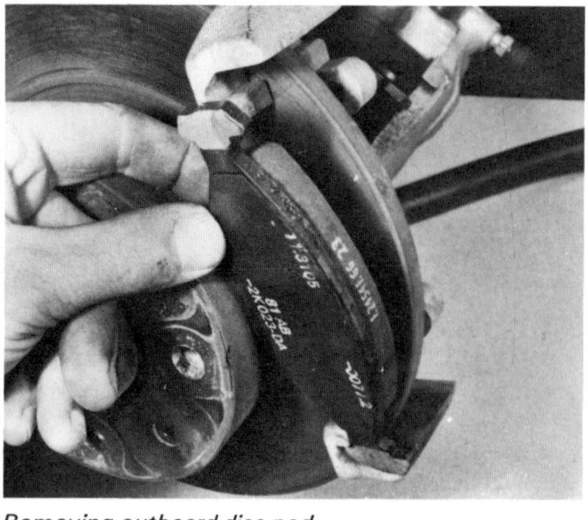

Removing outboard disc pad

Fitting disc pad retaining clip

Apply the footbrake hard several times to position the pads against the disc and then check and top up the fluid in the master cylinder reservoir. Fit the road-wheels and lower the vehicle.

Avoid heavy braking (if possible) for the first hundred miles or so when new pads have been fitted. This is to allow them to bed in and reach full efficiency.

If the disc pads are the type of pads which incorporate wear sensors, then the operations are very similar to those just described in the preceding Section, but once the roadwheel is removed and before the caliper is dismantled, disconnect the multi-plug for the wear sensor lead and unclip the lead from the bleed screw.

When reassembling, once the inboard pad is located in the piston housing, feed the wear sensor lead through the opening in the caliper and then attach it to the bleed nipple clip.

Where the cable has become unwound, loosely coil the surplus wire so that slack is taken out yet enough flexibility (25mm/1 in) is still allowed for pad wear. The coiled wire must on no account be stretched.

7 *Check wear in rear brake shoe linings*

Note that the use of a torque wrench will be required when refitting the brake drum and adjusting the wheel bearings.

Due to the fact that the rear brake drums are combined with the hubs, which makes removal of the drums more complicated than is the case with detachable drums, inspection of the shoe linings can be carried out at the specified intervals by prising out the small inspection plug from the brake backplate, and observing the linings through the hole using a mirror. A minimum thickness of friction material must always be observed (1 mm/0.04 in) on the shoes; if it

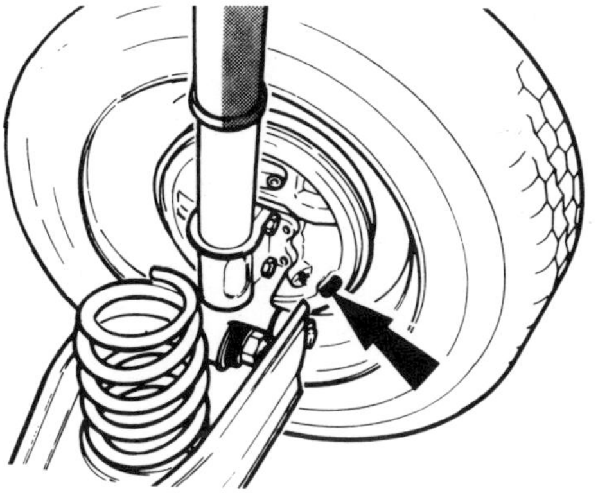

Rear brake shoe inspection plug

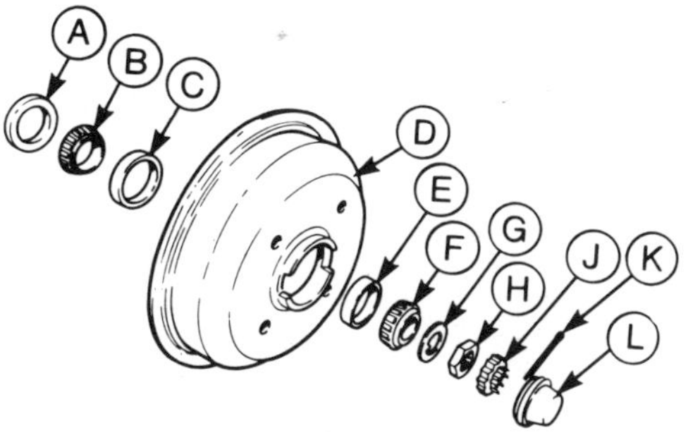

Rear hub/drum components

A	*Oil seal*	*G*	*Thrust washer*
B	*Tapered roller bearing (inner)*	*H*	*Nut*
		J	*Nut lock*
C	*Bearing track*	*K*	*Split pin*
D	*Hub/drum*	*L*	*Grease cap*
E	*Bearing track*		
F	*Tapered roller bearing (outer)*		

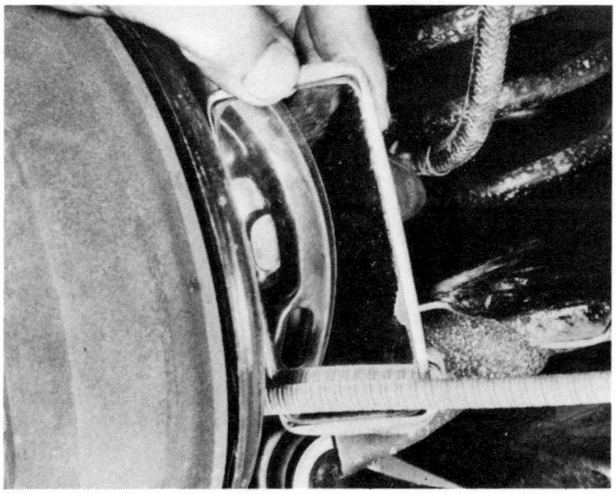

Checking rear brake lining with a mirror

Removing rear hub dust cap

Extracting rear hub split pin

Unscrewing rear hub nut

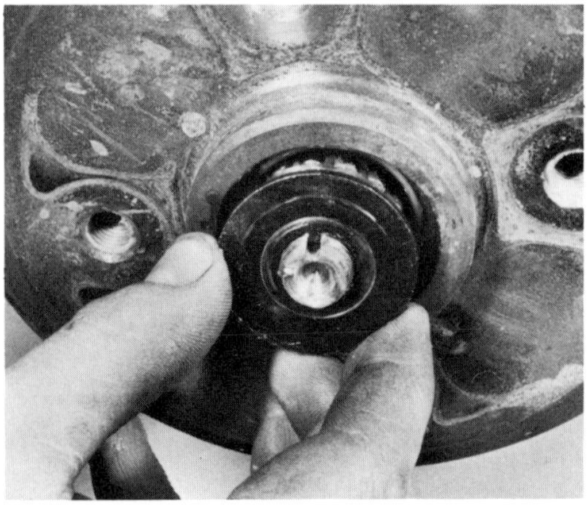
Removing rear hub thrust washer

Removing rear hub outer bearing

Rear hub/drum removed

Releasing brake shoe hold-down washer

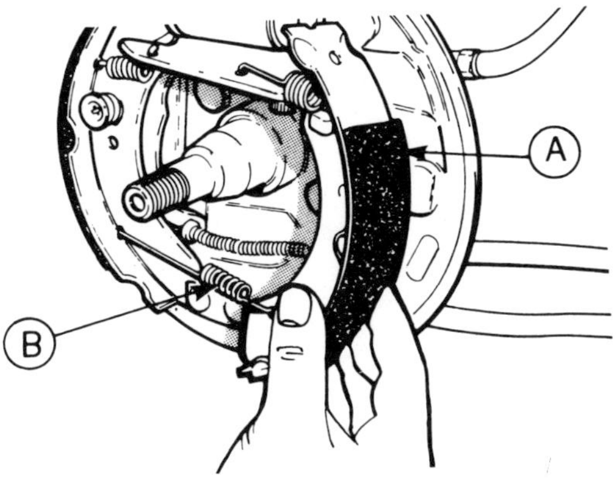

Withdrawing leading shoe

A Shoe B Spring

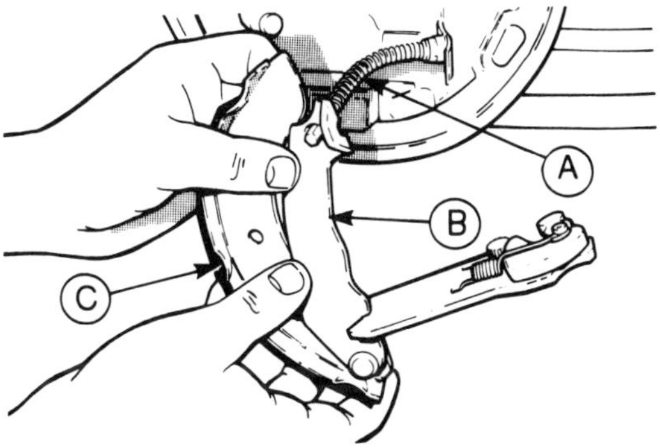

Handbrake cable attachment to shoe

A Cable C Shoe
B Lever

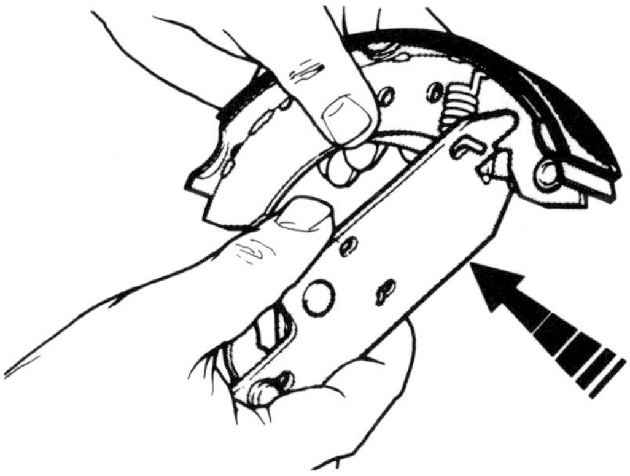

Separating trailing shoe from spacer strut

is worn down to this level, renew the shoes. Do not attempt to re-line shoes yourself but always obtain factory re-lined shoes. Renew the shoes in an axle set (four shoes), even if only one is worn to the minimum.

Slacken the roadwheel bolts, raise the rear of the vehicle and support it securely. Remove the road-wheels, then release the handbrake fully.

Tap off the hub dust cap, remove the split pin, nut lock, nut and thrust washer. Pull the hub/drum towards you and then push it back enough to be able to take the outer bearing from the spindle. Remove the hub/drum and brush out any dust, taking care not to inhale it.

Remove the shoe hold-down spring from the leading shoe. Do this by gripping the dished washer with a pair of pliers, depressing it and turning it through 90°. Remove the washer, spring and the hold-down post. Note the locations of the leading and trailing shoes and the cut-back of the linings at the leading ends. Pull the leading shoe outwards and upwards away from the backplate. Twist the shoe to unhook it from its return springs. If you have any doubt about remembering into which holes the springs engage, mark or sketch them. Remove the trailing shoe in a similar way, at the same time withdrawing the spacer strut. Release the end of the handbrake cable from the lever on the shoe. Finally disconnect the trailing shoe from the spacer strut by pulling the shoe outwards and twisting the shoe spring.

Commence reassembly by installing the trailing shoe. Do this by engaging the handbrake lever return spring to the shoe. Hook the spacer strut onto the spring and lever it into position. Locate the webs of the trailing shoe on the wheel cylinder and the fixed abutment, making sure that the lower end of the handbrake lever is correctly located on the face of the plastic plunger and not trapped behind it. Fit the trailing shoe hold-down post and spring.

Hold the leading shoe in position. Connect the larger shoe return spring at the lower (abutment) position between both shoes. Holding the leading shoe almost at right-angles to the backplate, connect the spring between it and the strut and then engage the bottom end of the shoe behind the abutment retainer plate. Swivel the shoe towards the backplate so that the cut-out in its web passes over the quadrant lever. Fit the shoe hold-down post, spring and washer.

Centralise the shoes within the backplate by tapping them if necessary with the hand, then fit the hub/drum and slide the outer bearing onto the spindle.

Fit the thrust washer and nut and, whilst rotating the drum, tighten the nut to a torque of 24 Nm (17 lbf ft). Unscrew the nut one half a turn and then screw the nut up again, but this time only finger tight. Without altering the position of the nut, fit the nut lock so that suitable cut-outs align with the split pin hole. Insert a new split pin and bend the ends *around* the spindle, *not* over the end of it or the pin may rub on the inside of the dust cap.

Depress the brake pedal hard several times to actuate the self-adjusting mechanism and to bring the shoes up close to the drum. Refit the roadwheel and lower the vehicle to the floor.

8 Clean fuel pump

This is the only work which can be carried out on the fuel pump. To do this, place a piece of rag around the pump body to catch the fuel which will drain out when the cover is removed.

Unscrew and remove the single cover screw and lift off the cover. Take out the rubber sealing ring and the filter screen from inside the cover.

Clean the screen by brushing it in clean fuel, then fit it into the cover, noting the projections on some screens which centralise it. Fit the sealing ring. If it is not in good order, renew it. Locate the cover on the pump body. On some pumps, the cover is correctly installed when the notch in the cover engages in the groove in the pump body. Screw in the retaining screw, but do not overtighten it provided it is making a good seal.

9 Check steering joints for wear and gaiters for deterioration

Regularly check the condition of the steering gear bellows and the tie-rod balljoint dust excluders. If split, they must be renewed immediately, and in the case of the steering gear, the lubricant cleared out and fresh injected by your dealer.

With an assistant turning the steering wheel from side-to-side, check for lost motion at the tie-rod end balljoints. If evident, have the balljoints renewed as no repair or lubrication is possible.

When the front wheels are raised, avoid turning the steering wheel rapidly from lock-to-lock. This could cause hydraulic pressure build-up, with consequent damage to the bellows.

10 Check the tightness of the roadwheel bolts

There is no need to attempt to shear the bolts by using excessive force as some people do. Apart from straining the threads, the dished recesses in the wheels will gradually become deformed if the bolts are continually overtightened. Using a reasonable amount of strength on the angled wrench supplied is sufficient, or if a torque wrench is available, tighten to 59 lbf ft (80 Nm).

11 Check drivebelt tension and condition

The tension should be checked as detailed in item 1 of the schedule given for the end of the first 1500 miles (2500 km) on new vehicles. The drivebelt should also be carefully inspected for condition. If it shows signs of obvious wear – fraying, cracks or splits etc – it should be renewed now rather than waiting for it to fail on the road. This will invariably happen on a dark rainy night in the middle of nowhere with no tools or spare belt in the car! So change it now if any of these defects are obvious.

To remove a belt, slacken the alternator mounting bolts and the bolts on the adjuster link, push the alternator in towards the engine and slip the belt from the pulleys.

Fit the new belt by slipping it over the pulley rims while the alternator is still loose on its mountings. Never be tempted to remove or fit a belt by prising it over a pulley without releasing the alternator. Either the pulley will be distorted or the alternator or coolant pump will be damaged.

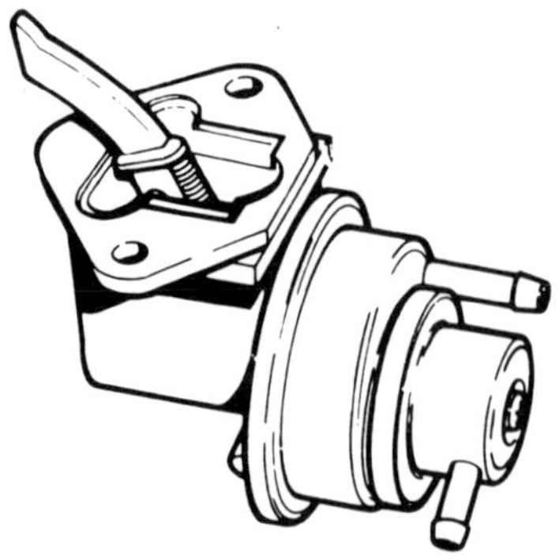

Fuel pump (ohv engine)

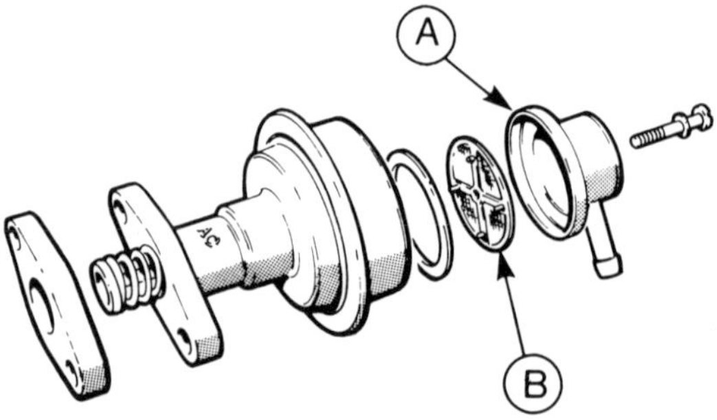

Fuel pump (CVH engine)

A Cover B Filter screen

The belt should now be tensioned using the details given in the aforementioned schedule.

12 Check for fluid leaks

Again, reference should be made to the schedule for the end of the first 1500 miles (2500 km) on new vehicles; details are listed under item 6.

13 Check brake hydraulic system components for condition

The braking system should be checked over carefully for any evidence of leakage. Check that the rigid brake pipes are not badly corroded or damaged by impact with flying stones, chafing etc. The flexible brake hoses should be carefully checked for cracking, cuts, chafing or leakage at their end fittings. Gently bend the hoses by hand and observe whether any fine cracks in the outer covering become apparent. If this condition is evident, the hose should be renewed by your dealer.

14 Check engine idle speed

Refer once again to the schedule for the end of the first 1500 miles (2500 km) on new vehicles; details are given under item 5.

15 Check tyres for wear or damage

This is a visual exercise. First check that the tread depth is at least 1.0 mm. Even this amount of tread will not provide much better traction than a bald tyre under severe braking or cornering, and it is far safer to fit new tyres rather than wait until the legal requirement is no longer met.

Examine the sidewalls; this means the inside ones as well. Any sign of blisters, bulges or cuts means the tyre must be scrapped.

If you find a nail or sharp object embedded in the tread, don't immediately pull it out, but mark round the object with chalk so that the tyre repairer will be able to locate the puncture quickly.

The life of your tyres can be increased by not rubbing against kerbs, avoiding bumping up kerbs and always maintaining the correct pressures.

Radial ply tyres are fitted as original equipment and this type of tyre should always be specified at time of renewal. Steel radials will give a longer life than textile ones.

Always have the wheels balanced. If it is desired to move the position of the roadwheels to minimise tyre wear, only move them front to rear or rear to front of the same side of the vehicle – never from side to side with radial tyres.

EVERY 12 000 MILES (20 000 KM)

(In addition to the items specified in the previous schedule)

The following items may be required:

Spark plugs, contact breaker points (mechanical system only), transmission oil.

1 Check valve clearances

This only applies if your car is an ohv engined model – CVH models have self-adjusting hydraulic tappets

This should be carried out as detailed in item 3 of the schedule given for the end of the first 1500 miles (2500 km) on new vehicles.

2 Renew spark plugs

Although the spark plugs will (hopefully) have been cleaned and regapped at their specified intervals, they should be renewed after 12 000 miles (20 000 km) use. However good they look, their performance will have deteriorated to the point where they are adversely affecting economy and power output. Refer to the 6000 mile (10 000 km) schedule for details of removal and refitting.

3 Renew distributor contact breaker points

On 1.1 litre engined vehicles, the contact breaker points of the mechanical ignition system distributor should be renewed as soon as their contact faces become eroded or burned to any extent.

Disconnect the leads from the spark plugs, prise down the distributor cap clips or remove the screws, and place the cap and leads to one side. Remove the rotor arm.

Pull off the contact breaker LT lead from the points. Unscrew and remove the screw from the fixed contact arm. Take great care not to drop the screw into the interior of the distributor; if necessary, cover the openings in the baseplate with rag before starting to remove the screw. With the screw removed, lift out the contact breaker assembly.

Dressing the points on a strip of emery cloth is not recommended and they should be renewed if they are in poor condition or they have completed their specified period of service.

Fit the new contact breaker set, but leave the securing screw loose at this stage until the gap has been set using feeler blades.

Apply a spanner to the crankshaft pulley bolt and turn the crankshaft until the distributor points are fully open, with the heel of the cam follower on the highest point of one of the lobes of the cam. Using feeler blades, check the points gap. If the blade is not a sliding fit, release the screw at the fixed contact so that the contact will move stiffly, and adjust the gap. Retighten the screw, refit the rotor and cap. Take care not to contaminate the points with oil from the feeler gauges.

The points gap on Bosch distributors should be between 0.016 and 0.020 in (0.4 and 0.5 mm) and

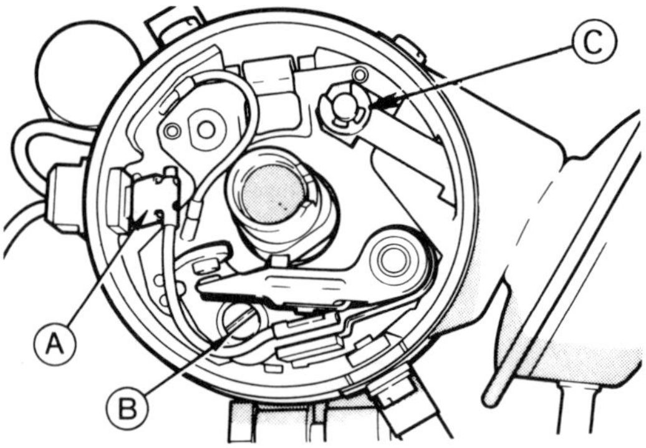

Contact breaker points (Bosch distributor/ohv engine)

A LT lead connector
B Securing screw
C Vacuum advance strut circlip

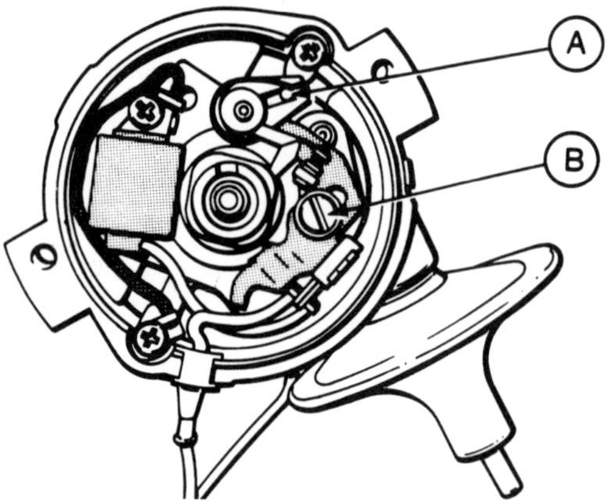

Contact breaker points (Lucas distributor/CVH engine)

A Secondary movement cam
B Securing screw

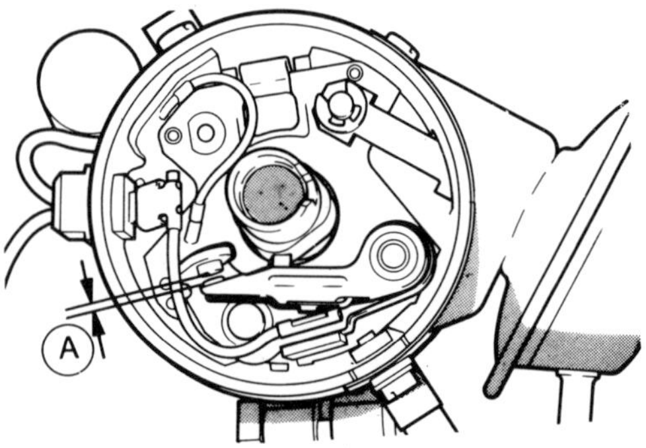

Contact breaker points gap (A)

on Lucas distributors 0.016 to 0.024 in (0.4 to 0.6 mm).

On Lucas distributors, make sure that the secondary movement cam is engaged with its pin, and that both washers are refitted with the securing screw. Apply a little high melting-point grease to the distributor cam.

Refit the rotor arm and the distributor cap and reconnect the spark plug leads.

Check and adjust the dwell angle and the ignition timing as described earlier under the 6000 mile (10 000 km) service schedule.

4 Lubricate distributor and clean cap and leads

This work will of course be carried out at the same time as the contact breaker points are renewed. Add one drop only of engine oil to the contact breaker pivot post and two drops to the felt pad exposed when the rotor arm is removed from the distributor shaft. Greasing the distributor shaft cam has already been done during contact breaker points renewal (preceding sub-section).

Now wipe out the distributor cap and check the condition of the central carbon contact and the high tension lead contacts. If these are eroded or burned severely, renew the cap.

Examine the surface of the cap for tiny cracks. If evident, the cap must be renewed as they can provide conductance paths for electrical current and this will make the engine run roughly, or possibly prevent it from starting.

Finally, wipe all grease from the HT leads and make sure that their ends are pushed fully into their distributor sockets and onto the spark plug terminals.

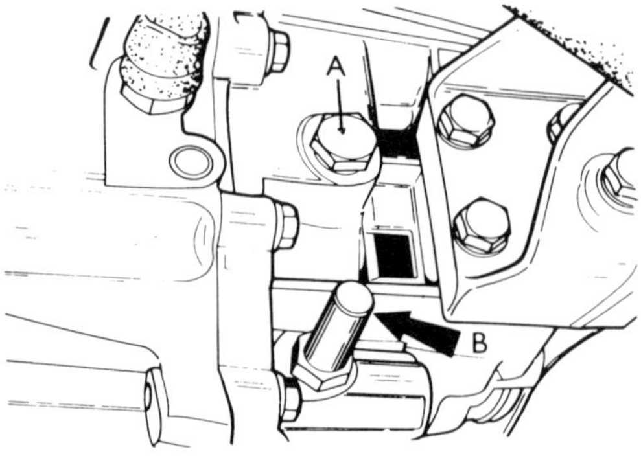

Transmission filler/level plug (A) and selector cap nut (for draining) (B)

Topping up transmission

Exhaust expansion box mounting

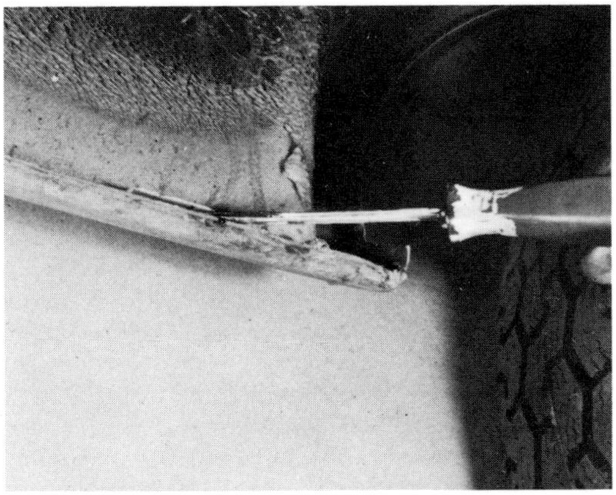

Clearing a sill drain hole

Clearing a door drain hole

5 Check transmission oil level and top up

A combined level/filler plug is fitted and the correct oil level is established when the oil is just seen to be running out of the plug hole when the vehicle is on level ground.

Regular oil changing is not specified by the manufacturers, but the oil can be drained if necessary (after a high mileage or after transversing a flooded road for example) by removing the selector shaft locking mechanism cap nut. Take care not to lose the spring and interlock pin which will be ejected.

6 Check condition of driveshaft gaiters

To do this, raise the front of the vehicle and support securely with the roadwheels off the ground. Now turn each of the front roadwheels while the driveshaft bellows are carefully examined for splits or general deterioration. Where they are not in perfect condition, have them renewed immediately.

7 Check exhaust system for corrosion

There are two reasons for the rapid rusting and corrosion in an exhaust system. Water being sprayed onto the hot outer surfaces creates rust on the outside, while acids and condensation produced by combustion corrode the interior. The application of high temperature-resistant paint to the outside of the exhaust system may help to preserve it. A vehicle which only covers short journeys without the engine ever getting really hot will suffer greater exhaust internal corrosion than one that is used mainly for long trips.

If the vehicle is likely to be kept for a long time, then investment in a stainless steel exhaust system may be worth considering.

Wire brush the exhaust pipes and silencer. Probe any severely rusted areas with a screwdriver. If the metal collapses then that section at least, if not the complete system, will have to be renewed. At the same time check the condition of the system flexible mountings and renew as necessary.

8 Lubricate controls and clear drain holes

This is a simple yet essential service operation. Apply engine oil to the door and hatchback or tailgate hinges and locks. Partially insert the key in the lock cylinders and then let a little thin oil run down the key into the lock.

Oil the carburettor control linkage, bonnet hinges and catch.

Probe the door and body sill drain holes to provide good drainage for any accumulations of water.

9 Check rear hub bearing adjustment

This adjustment will normally only be required if, when the rear of the vehicle is raised and the top and bottom of the roadwheel are gripped and 'rocked', a slight movement can be detected in the bearings. Unless a torque wrench is available, this job should be entrusted to your dealer.

Raise the vehicle and support it securely on stands, then remove the roadwheel. Using a hammer and cold chisel, tap off the dust cap from the end of the hub. Extract the split pin and take off the nut retainer.

Tighten the hub nut to a torque of 24 Nm (17 lbf ft), at the same time rotating the roadwheel in an anti-clockwise direction. Unscrew the nut one half a turn and then tighten it only finger tight. Fit the nut retainer so that two of its slots line up with the split pin hole. Insert a new split pin, bending the end *around* the nut, *not* over the end of the stub axle. Tap the dust cap into position.

Repeat the operations on the opposite hub, refit the roadwheels and lower the vehicle to the floor.

10 Check headlamp beam alignment

Apart from being an annual test requirement, correctly aligned headlamp beams will benefit not only you but other road users. Adjustment of the beams is very definitely a job for your dealer or service station.

EVERY 24 000 MILES (40 000 km)

(In addition to the items specified in the previous schedule).

The following items may be required:

Crankcase emission filter (CVH only), emission control orifice (ohv only), air cleaner element.

1 Service crankcase ventilation system

Disconnect the system hoses from the crankcase, rocker cover and air cleaner, and clean them out. If a noticeable quantity of sludge or emulsified oil is present, especially in cold weather, this indicates that the engine is running too cool. If this is the case, consult your dealer for advice. Reconnect the hoses.

On CVH engines, the crankcase emission filter must be renewed. This is removed by detaching both pipes from the filter body and pulling the filter from the air cleaner unit. The new filter is fitted using the reverse sequence, ensuring that the rubber seal is correctly seated.

On ohv engines, the emission control orifice in the oil filler cap should be cleaned or renewed. The orifice is removed by twisting and pulling out of the filler cap after disconnecting the middle pipe to give access. Take care not to damage the body of the orifice during removal. Clean the orifice in paraffin and allow it to dry. Don't poke bits of wire or suchlike into the orifice to remove any hard deposits, or the calibration will be upset. If they won't wash out in

Connecting crankcase ventilation front hose

Connecting crankcase ventilation rear hose

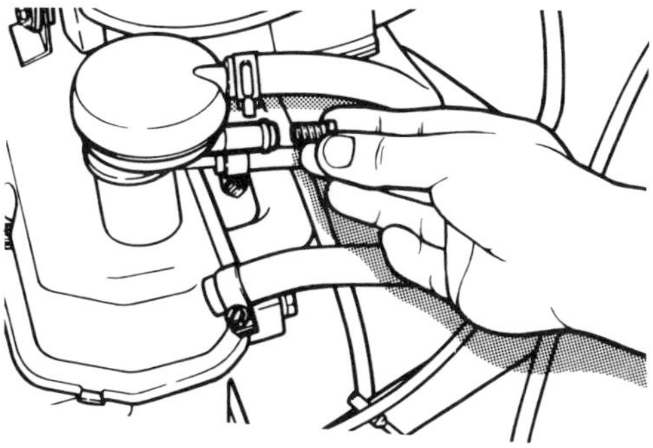

Renewing control orifice in filler cap (ohv engines only)

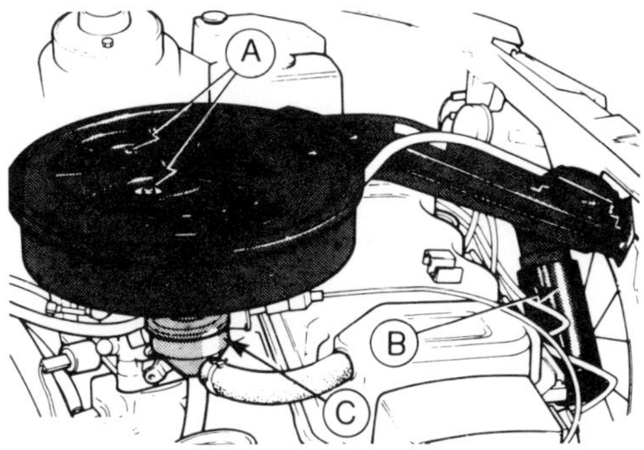

Crankcase ventilation system (CVH engine)

A Screws *C Emission filter*
B Hot air intake

paraffin, renew the control orifice. Reconnect the pipe to the oil filler cap after fitting.

2 Renew air cleaner element

This is a most essential operation in order to maintain maximum fuel economy.

Most models have a circular air cleaner, but versions with a dual venturi carburettor have an oval one. The following description applies to both types.

Unscrew and remove the lid securing screws and lift off the lid.

Remove and discard the air cleaner element and wipe out the interior of the casing. Place the new element in position and refit the lid.

EVERY TWO YEARS

Renew antifreeze coolant mixture

Never operate the vehicle with plain water in the cooling system. Apart from the danger of freezing during winter conditions, an important secondary purpose of antifreeze is to inhibit the formation of rust and to reduce corrosion. This is particularly important with the CVH engine which has an alloy cylinder head.

Use a reliable brand of antifreeze with a glycol base – never one containing methanol which will evaporate during use. Renew the coolant at the specified intervals. Although the antifreeze properties of the coolant will remain indefinitely, the effectiveness of the rust and corrosion inhibitors will gradually weaken. Even in climates where antifreeze is not required, never use plain water, but use one of the branded corrosion inhibitors available. A solution of 45% antifreeze will protect the system adequately against all danger from frost, rust and corrosion.

It is preferable to drain the system when the coolant is cold. If it must be drained when hot, release the pressure cap very slowly, having first covered it with a cloth to avoid any possibility of scalding.

Removing air cleaner lid screw

Removing air cleaner element

Set the heater control to maximum heat position. Place a container under the radiator and release the bottom hose. Allow the system to drain. Provided the coolant is of the correct antifreeze mixture then no flushing should be necessary and the system can be refilled immediately as described below. Where the system has been neglected, however, and rust or sludge is evident at draining, then the system should be flushed through with a cold water hose inserted into the thermostat housing (thermostat removed) until the water flows clean from the disconnected bottom hose and the radiator. In severe cases, the drain plug on the cylinder block can be unscrewed to assist sludge removal and flushing.

When the cooolant is being changed, it is recommended that the overflow pipe is disconnected from the expansion tank and the coolant drained from the tank. If the interior of the tank is dirty, remove it and thoroughly clean it out. Evidence of oil within the expansion tank may indicate a leaking cylinder head gasket.

Reconnect the radiator and expansion tank hoses, and refit the cylinder block drain plug (if removed). Using the correct antifreeze mixture, fill the system through the thermostat housing filler neck slowly until the coolant is nearly overflowing. Wait a few moments for trapped air to escape and add more coolant. Repeat until the level does not drop and refit the cap. Pour similar strength coolant into the expansion tank up to the level marked and fit the cap. Start the engine and run it to normal operating temperature. Once it has cooled, check and carry out any final topping up *to the expansion tank only.*

EVERY 3 YEARS

Renew brake hydraulic fluid

Brake hydraulic fluid has the unfortunate characteristic of being able to absorb moisture from the atmosphere. For this reason, it is recommended that the old fluid is bled out of the system and new fluid added as a safety precaution against corrosion and general deterioration of the system internal components. Leave this work to your dealer, and at the same time discuss with him the advisability of renewing the seals in all the hydraulic assemblies.

AS AND WHEN NECESSARY

Handbrake adjustment

Adjustment of the handbrake is normally automatic by means of the self-adjusting mechanism working on the rear brake shoes. However, due to cable stretch, occasional inspection of the handbrake adjusters is recommended. Adjustment must be carried out if the movement of the control lever becomes excessive.

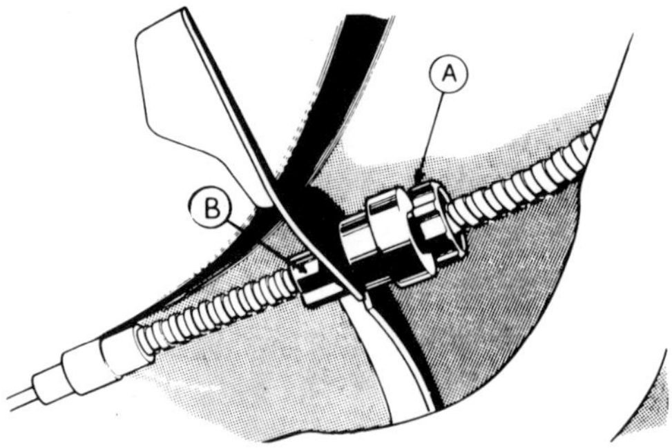

Handbrake cable adjuster (earlier type illustrated)
A Nut B Sleeve

Make sure that the handbrake is fully off. Check for movement at the adjuster plungers at the brake backplates. If the total movement (both sides added together) is between 1.0 and 2.5 mm (0.04 and 0.09 in), then adjustment is satisfactory. If there is no movement or if it exceeds that specified, adjust in the following way.

Up to early 1982

Make sure that the keyed sleeve on the cable conduit is engaged in its bracket slot. Unlock the adjusting nut by levering between the shoulders of nut and sleeve. Now turn the adjuster nut to eliminate slackness from the cable so that it is just possible to rotate the adjustment plungers. Give the adjuster nut a further $\frac{1}{4}$ to $\frac{1}{2}$ turn. Apply the handbrake control lever fully to seat the adjuster nut against its sleeve.

If adjustment of the cable does not alter the plunger movement then the handbrake cable must be binding or the brake mechanism is at fault.

Early 1982 onwards

All Escort models produced after January 1982 are fitted with revised handbrake cables and a modified adjuster. The revised cables can be identified by the coarser wound outer cable and threaded adjusting sleeve incorporating finger grips.

Slacken off the handbrake cable locknut, then unscrew the adjusting sleeve until the cable is slack. Now apply the footbrake vigorously to ensure full adjustment of the automatic adjusters. Screw the adjusting sleeve into contact with the abutment bracket, and continue tightening until the total movement of both adjustment plungers added together is between 0.5 and 2.0 mm (0.02 and 0.08 in). Tighten the locknut against the adjusting sleeve by hand until the tangs of the locknut engage securely in the indents of the sleeve. Do not tighten the locknut any further.

After adjustment ensure that the rear wheels are still free to turn without any trace of binding.

OTHER REGULAR SERVICING

If you carry out the procedures we've detailed so far, at more or less the prescribed intervals of mileage or time, then you'll have gone a long way towards getting the best out of your Ford in terms of both performance and long life. That's the good news. The other kind is that there are always other areas, not dealt with in regular servicing schedules, where neglect can spell trouble.

We reckon a bit of extra time spent on your car at the beginning and end of the winter will be well repaid in terms of peace of mind and prevention of trouble. The suggested attentions which follow have therefore been divided into Spring and Autumn sections – but there's nothing to prevent you doing them more frequently if you like!

SPRING

We've put this one first as it's less depressing than Autumn – though there's probably more work involved!

Underside of car

In Spring, we venture to suggest, the owner's fancy lightly turns to thoughts of cleaning off all the accumulated muck of winter from underneath the car. Without a shadow of doubt, the best time to clean underneath is the worst time from the discomfort point of view – that is, when the car's been driven in the wet and all the dirt's nicely softened up. So let's talk first about the easiest way out – steam cleaning or pressure washing.

These aren't D-I-Y jobs, and can only be done at larger garages, usually those which undertake body repair jobs. You may feel this method's unnecessarily expensive, but it's generally preferable to grovelling about underneath and getting filthy and uncomfortable doing it yourself. However, for the owner who really wants to do it by hand, here goes ....

You'll need paraffin or a water-soluble solvent, water (and preferably a hose), a wire brush, a scraper and a stiff-bristle brush. If you think the car floor may leak, remove the carpets or they'll get wet; this will also help you pinpoint the places where water's getting in.

To start with, jack the car up as high as possible, preferably at one side or one end. For your own safety, support it on ramps or concrete or wooden blocks and chock the wheels which are on the ground. Unless both rear wheels are raised, also apply the handbrake; similarly, unless both front wheels are off the ground engage first or reverse gear.

Now get underneath (you've put it off as long as you can!) and cover the brake discs and calipers with polythene bags to stop mud and water getting into them. Next loosen any encrusted dirt and, working from one end or one side, scrape or brush it away. The paraffin or solvent can be used where there's oil contamination. After all the brushing and scraping, a final wash down with the hose will remove the last of the dirt and mud.

You can now check for leaks in the floor; if you find any, dry the area carefully then use a mastic type sealer to plug the offending gap. Hollow sections of doors and bodywork can be sprayed or brush-painted with a rust-inhibitor to provide some extra protection. If there are signs of the underseal breaking away, this is a good opportunity to patch it up. Undersealing paint is available in spray cans or tins from accessory shops; one small point about putting the stuff on though, and that's to make sure the area is clean and dry, otherwise you're wasting your time.

While you're underneath, have a good look round for signs of rusting. Likely places are the body sills and floor panels, and if you do find any rust have a word with the local Ford man or body repair shop before things get too bad.

Bodywork

This too will have suffered from all the muck and salt that's around during the winter, and there's no better time to wash it thoroughly and check for stone chips and rust spots. You're bound to find some, despite the regular washing you've given the car – or meant to – throughout the winter. Treat as for rusty scratches (see *Body Beautiful).*

After the touch-up has thoroughly hardened, it's worth giving the car a good polish to prepare it for the long, hot summer ahead (well, there's no harm in hoping). If you're feeling really energetic you could do the interior as well, but the most important cleaning jobs are now done.

AUTUMN

With winter on the way, your car's electrical system is going to take much more of a beating than it has during the last few months. Now – and not on a dark night miles from anywhere in a snowstorm – is the time to check the vital components.

Battery

Ensure this is topped up correctly.
Check and clean as necessary.

Alternator/water pump drivebelt

Adjust and check for fraying.

Lights

Check operation.

Renew any failed bulbs or check for faults as necessary.

Wipers/washers

These are going to get a lot of use, so check the wiper arms and blades. Top up washer reservoir and check operation.

Cooling system

Check all hoses.

Drain, flush and refill system with new antifreeze mixture if there is any doubt about the strength of the old coolant.

Tyres

Check tread and condition. Remember that you may well be driving in slippery conditions.

Bodywork

Finally, if you've got any energy left, wash the car and polish it thoroughly to help protect the paint against the winter elements.

Body Beautiful

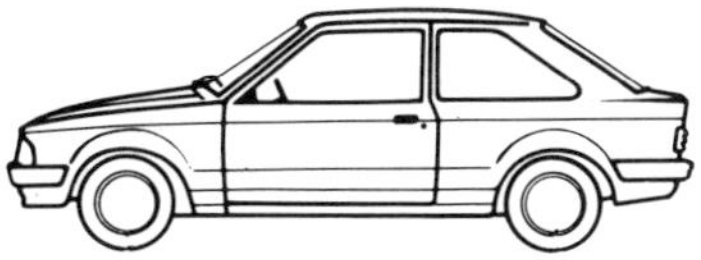

If you've bought this book intending to do all the routine servicing of your car yourself, then you'll surely want to keep the bodywork and inside of the car looking good too. For anyone who doesn't here's how to do it anyway ...

It's always a good idea to clean the interior first; this way you won't get the dust all over your nicely polished exterior – or the car's! Begin by removing all the contents, not forgetting the odds and ends in the pockets and glovebox. Then take out all the mats and carpets, which should be shaken and brushed, or better still vacuum-cleaned. If they need further cleaning, this can be done with a carpet shampoo, but let them dry thoroughly before you put them back. Any underfelt should be taken out and shaken too, but don't try washing this or it may end up in rather more pieces than you started with.

If the carpets should just happen to be in such a bad state of decay that they don't merit cleaning, why not get yourself a decent set of replacements? You can get kits tailored for your particular model from specialist firms, and they're quite reasonably priced.

The inside of the car can now be cleaned with a brush and dustpan, or again preferably a vacuum-cleaner. If the flex on the vacuum won't stretch to the car (and the car won't squeeze through the front door!) it might be worth thinking about investing in one of the small 12 volt hand vacuums which can be attached to your car battery – your accessorty shop can probably show you one.

Seat and trim materials can be wiped over with warm water containing a little washing-up liquid, but for best results (particularly if they're very dirty) use one of the proprietary upholstery cleaners which are specially made for the job. An old nail brush will help to remove ingrained marks, but won't splash too much about and do wipe the surfaces dry afterwards with a clean cloth, leaving the windows open to speed up drying. The carpets can be put back when they're quite dry, making sure they're properly fitted around the controls etc.

You have to be careful about cleaning car windows, especially the windscreen, with some household products as these can leave a smeary film. Water containing a few drops of ammonia is probably best, but any stubborn marks and smears can be removed with methylated spirit; finish off with a chamois leather squeezed as dry as possible.

Just in case you should think that's it, there's still the luggage compartment to be dealt with. Take out that collection of junk that seems to have grown every time you open the lid, and get busy with brush or vacuum cleaner again. While you're at it, if you must carry all that stuff around, now's the time to try and stow it so it doesn't rattle any more!

Now you can pause for a moment – make a well earned cup of tea perhaps – and take a critical look at the interior. Are there any nicks or tears in the seats or other trim? Is the headlining drooping or peeling? Some excellent products can now be obtained for repairs such as these. One of the most useful is probably the vinyl repair kit, which comes in various colours and consists of a quantity of 'liquid vinyl' and some sheets of texturing material. The liquid is applied to a split or hole in a plastic seat or piece of trim, smoothed like body filler, and allowed to set. It's then blended into the surrounding area by selecting the best matching pattern from the graining material supplied, placing this over the repair and rubbing with a hot iron; the pattern is then embossed in the repaired area. This type of repair's equally successful, incidentally, on vinyl roofs if your car happens to have one.

For larger splits or tears it may be necessary to cut a piece of matching material from somewhere that doesn't show, apply some suitable adhesive to it and work it under the edges of the tear, pressing these together as neatly as possible once the glue has become tacky enough. Any loose headlining or trim can also be stuck in place – but make sure you get an adhesive that's suitable for PVC or vinyl.

Once you've got the seats in a reasonable state of cleanliness and repair, why not consider seat covers? Like the carpets, they're available from specialist firms to suit your car and are a worthwhile buy in view of the protection they give.

If you use the car regularly and you've got the time and inclination, it should really be washed every week, either by hand (preferably using a hosepipe) or by taking advantage of the local car-wash if there is one. Whichever method you choose (assuming you wash your car at all!) we don't think we need tell you how to do it – but remember it's never a good idea to just wipe over a very dirty car, whether wet or dry; you might as well sandpaper it!

Two or three times a year (even once is better than not at all) a good silicone or wax polish can be used on the paintwork. We don't know which of the many makes you'll use, so we can only recommend you to follow the maker's instructions closely so that you do see a reward for your efforts. Chrome parts are best cleaned with a special chrome cleaner; ordinary metal polish will attack the finish.

If the paint's beginning to lose its gloss or colour, and ordinary polishing doesn't seem to help it, it will be worth condsidering the use of a polish with a mild 'cutting' action to remove what is, in effect, a surface layer of dead paint. Your friendly neighbourhood accessory shop man will advise on a suitable type.

The remainder of this Chapter describes how to keep your car's bodywork and paintwork in good condition by dealing with scratches, and more major damage too, as they occur. A number of repair aids and materials are referred to, most of them essential if you're to achieve good results. They should all be available, together with free advice, from good motor accessory shops.

Keeping paintwork up to scratch

With superficial scratches (the sort only other people seem to get) where they don't penetrate down to the metal, you'll be glad to hear that repair can be very simple. Lightly rub the area with a paintwork renovator or a fine cutting paste to remove any loose paint from the scratch and to clean off any polish. Rinse the area with plenty of clean water and allow to dry. Apply touch-up paint to the scratch using a fine brush, and continue to build up the paint by several applications, allowing each to dry, until it's level with the surrounding area. Allow the new paint at least two weeks to harden, then use the paintwork renovator or cutting paste again to blend into the original. Now a good polish can be used.

When you've got a scratch that's penetrated right through to the metal, causing rusting, you need a different technique. Use your Scout knife to remove any loose rust from the bottom of the scratch, then paint on a rust-inhibiting paint to prevent it from spreading. You'll probably now need to apply cellulose body stopper paste – use a rubber or nylon applicator or a knife, but don't borrow one from the kitchen as you'll have a job cleaning it!

The paste can be thinned down if necessary using cellulose thinners. Before it hardens, it's a good idea to wrap a piece of smooth cotton rag round the end of your finger, dip it in thinners and quickly sweep it across the filled scratch. This ensures that the area is very slightly hollowed and allows the paint to be built up to the correct level as described earlier.

Dealing with dents

When your car's bodywork gets a deep depression, you'll have one too. There's no reason why even fairly large dents can't be tackled successfully by the D-I-Y owner, especially using the excellent body repair materials now available. So cheer up, and let's see what can be done.

The first step is to try to pull the dented metal out to bring it more or less back to the original level. Don't expect to make a perfect job of this – you won't; the metal has stretched and 'work-hardened' which makes it a virtually impossible job. Try to bring the level up to about $\frac{1}{8}$ inch below the surrounding area; obviously, with shallow dents you can bypass this bit. If the underside of the dent can be got at, try hammering it out gently from behind using a hammer with a wooden or plastic head. You'll need to hold a fairly heavy hardwood block on the outside of the dent; this absorbs the impact of the hammer blows and helps to stop the metal being dented in the opposite direction!

If you've got a dent in a completely enclosed body section, or there's something else preventing you from getting behind it, a different approach is needed. Try to screw up enough courage to drill several small holes through the metal in the dent, particularly in the deeper parts. Now screw in several self-tapping screws so that they get a good bite, and either pull on the heads with pliers, or wrap some heavy gauge steel wire round them and pull this. Brace yourself in case something gives suddenly or you may dent your own bodywork!

Now to remove the paint from the damaged area. This is best done using a power drill and abrasive disc, but if you've got the time and energy you can use elbow-grease and abrasive paper. Don't forget to remove the paint from an inch or so of the surrounding good paintwork, too, so that everything blends in nicely. Now score the metal surface with a screwdriver or the tang of a file to provide a good key for the filler which you're going to have to apply, in case you didn't know. Now, to finish off the repair, refer to the filling and spraying section at the end of this Chapter.

Rust holes and gashes

If there's any paint left on the affected area, remove it as described above so that you can get a good idea of just how bad the problem is. If there's more rust or fresh air than good metal, now's the time to consider whether a replacement panel would be more appropriate; this is a body shop job beyond the scope of this book.

If things don't seem that bad and you're prepared to have a go at doing the job yourself, remove all the fittings from the surrounding area except those which may help to give a good guide to what the shape should be (eg headlamp shells). Now, get a hacksaw blade or a pair of snips and cut out all the loose and badly affected metal. Hammer the edges inwards so thaty you've got a recessed area to build up on.

Wire brush the edges to remove any powdery rust, then paint over with a rust inhibitor; if you can get to the back, do the same to that. You're now going to fill the hole with something, but unfortunately just anything won't do. The best bets are zinc gauze or aluminium tape. The gauze is probably the favourite for a large hole. Cut a piece slightly larger than the hole to be filled, then position it in the hole so that its edges are below the level of the surrounding bodywork. If necessary, hold it in place with a few blobs of filler paste. For small or narrow holes you can use the aluminium tape which is sold by the roll. Pull off a piece and trim to the approximate size and shape required. If there's backing paper, peel it off (it sticks better that way!) and place the tape over the hole; if necessary, pieces can be overlapped at the edges. Burnish down the edges of the tape with a file handle or similar to make sure it's firmly adhering to the metal.

With the hole now blocked off, the affected area can be filled and sprayed as follows.

Filling and spraying

Many types of body filler are available, but generally speaking those proprietary kits which contain filler paste (or filler powder and resin liquid) and a separate hardener are best. You'll also need a flexible plastic or nylon applicator (usually supplied) for putting the mixture on with. Mix up a little of the filler on a piece of board or plastic (those plastic margarine tubs are ideal but do wash out all traces of the contents first!). Read the instructions carefully and don't make up too much at one go. You'll find you have to work fairly fast or the mixture will begin to set, especially if you've been generous with the hardener.

Apply the paste to the prepared hole or dent more or less to the correct level and contour, but don't try to shape it once it's become tacky or it'll pick up on the applicator. Layers should be built up at intervals until the final level's just proud of the surrounding bodywork.

When the filler has fully hardened, use a metal shaping plane or coarse file to remove the excess and obtain the final shape. Then follow with progressively finer grades of wet-or-dry abrasive paper starting with coarse, followed by medium, then fine (some manufacturers give 'grit' grades to their wet-or-dry paper – 40 is the coarsest, 400 is the finest). Always wrap the paper round a flat block if you're trying to get a flat surface, and keep it wet by rinsing in clean water or the filler and paint will clog up the abrasive surface.

At this point, the doctored area should be surrounded by a ring of bare metal, encircled by a feathered edge of good paintwork. Rinse it with plenty of clean water to get rid of all the paint and filler dust, and allow it to dry completely.

If you're happy with the surface you've obtained, then you're ready to apply some paint. First spray over the whole area with a light coat of grey primer. This will show up any surface imperfections which may need further treatment, and will also help you get the knack of spraying with an aerosol can before you start on the colour coats. Rub down the surface again, and if necessary use a little body stopper, as described for minor scratches, to fill any small imperfections. Repeat this spray-and-level procedure until you're satisfied with the finish; then wash down again and allow to dry.

The next stage is to apply the finishing coats, but first a word or two about the techniques involved. Paint spraying should be done in a warm, dry, windless, dust-free atmosphere – conditions not very readily available to most of us! You may be able to approach them artificially if you've got a large indoor workshop, but if you have to work outside you'll need to pick the day carefully. If you're working in your garage you'll probably need to 'lay' the dust on the floor by damping with water.

If the body repair's confined to a small patch, mask off the surrounding area to protect it from paint spray. Bodywork fittings (chrome strips, door handles

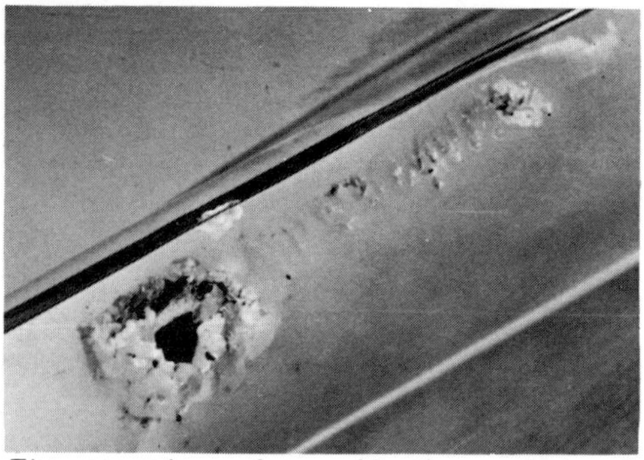

The procedure given with these photos is simplified; more comprehensive instructions will be found in the accompanying text. Typical rust damage is shown here, but the procedure for the repair of dents and gashes is similar.

First remove fittings from the immediate area and then remove loose rust and paint. A wire brush or abrasive disc mounted in a power drill is best, although the job can be done by hand. You need to be very thorough.

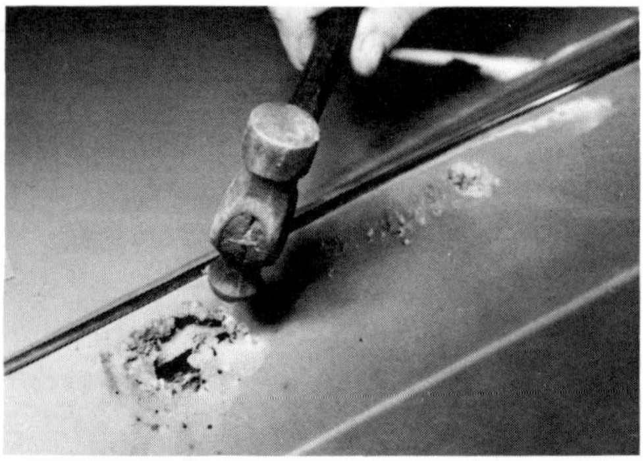

The edges of a hole should be tapped inwards with a hammer to provide a hollow for the filler. Having done this, apply rust inhibitor to the affected area (including the underside where possible) and allow this to dry thoroughly.

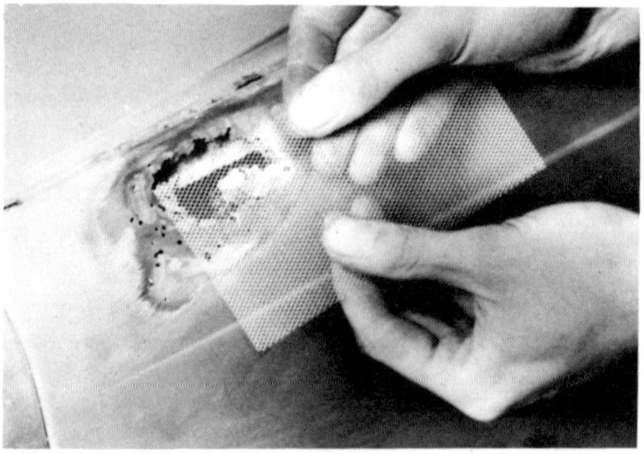

Before attempting to fill larger holes, block them off with suitable material. Metal tape can be used, but the picture shows a piece of aluminium gauze being sized up for use on this hole.

When mixing the body filler, follow the manufacturers' instructions very carefully. Mix thoroughly, don't mix too much at one go, and don't make it up until you're ready to start filling - modern fillers begin to harden very quickly!

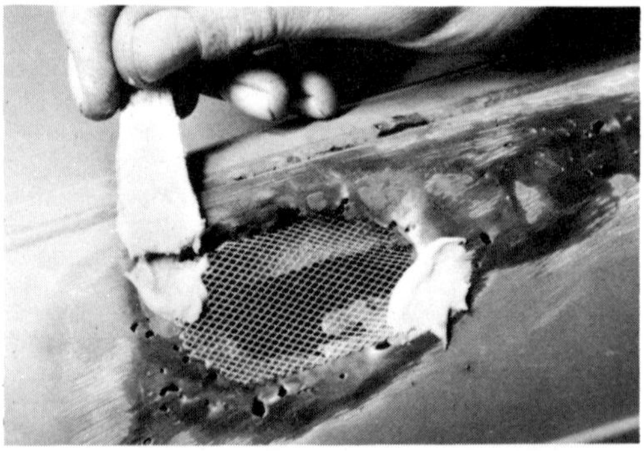

The tape or gauze used for backing up a hole can be secured in position with a few small blobs of filler paste. It's a good idea to mix a very small quantity for this purpose first.

After mixing the filler, apply it quickly with a flexible applicator, following the contours of the body. The filler should be built up in successive thin layers, the final one being just above the level of the surrounding bodywork.

A fairly coarse file or cutting tool is best for removing excess filler and for achieving the initial contour. Care must be taken not to overdo the filing or you'll hollow out the surface and have to fill it again!

A sanding block will now be needed; this can be made of wood as shown or a purpose-made rubber one can be purchased. Begin shaping the filler by using the block with progressively finer grades of dry abrasive paper, followed by ...

... wet and-dry paper, keeping both the work area and the paper wet. Rubbing down is complete when the filled area is 'feathered' into the surrounding painted areas, as shown; this final stage is achieved with the finest grade paper.

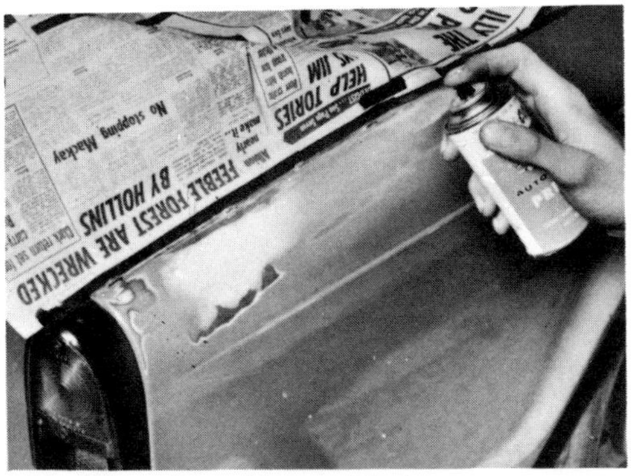

After thorough washing and drying, any necessary masking can be done and a coat of primer applied. Again, build this up with successive thin layers. Once the primer is dry it should be smoothed with very fine wet-and-dry paper.

The top coat of paint can now be applied, again in thin layers. Later a mild cutting paste can be used to blend it with the surrounding paint. Finish off with a good quality polish.

and the like) will need to be either masked or removed. If you're masking, use genuine masking tape and plenty of newspaper as necessary. Before starting to spray, shake the aerosol can thoroughly; then experiment on something (an old tin or similar will do – not the neighbours' car!) until you feel you can apply the paint smoothly. At the previous stage this wasn't too important, but now you're trying to get the best possible finish.

First cover the repair area with a thick coat of primer – not as one coat, but built up of several thin ones. When this is dry, using the finest wet-or-dry paper, rub down the surface until it's really smooth. Use plenty of water to keep the surface clean; when it's dry, spray on another primer coat and repeat the procedure.

Now for the top coat. Again the idea's to build up the paint thickness by several thin coats. Have a test spray first as this is a different aerosol, then commence spraying in the centre of the repair area. Using a circular motion, work gradually outwards towards the edges until the whole of the repair and about two inches of the surrounding original paint is covered. Remove all the masking material 10 to 15 minutes after you've finished spraying.

Now you can start to put away all the bits and pieces because it'll need about two weeks for the paint to harden completely. After this time time, using a paint renovator or a very fine cutting paste, blend the edges of the new paint into the original. Finally, apply a good wax or silicone polish, and hopefully you'll have a repair you're proud to own up to!

Adding 'pinstripes'

There are various kinds of self-adhesive body decor available for customising your car. Perhaps the neatest and most suitable of the 'add-on' variety are 'pinstripes', and we've mentioned these here as they may appeal to the owner who wants a cheap and simple way to improve the appearance of his or her car. 'Pinstripes' are adhesive tapes which come in different widths and colours, and as single or multi-stripes. Most have a backing paper which is peeled off as the stripe's applied.

When applying any of these self-adhesive tapes, first make sure the paintwork's clean by washing with warm water and a car shampoo or liquid detergent. Next clean up the surface with a very fine cutting paste or paintwork renovator, and wash down again. You can now apply the tape, but follow the directions carefully. Smooth it down with clean rag and, if necessary, prick out any small air bubbles with a pin. Try not to stretch the stripes as you put them on because they'll shrink slightly anyway; and wrap the ends round the panels so that they don't pull away at the edges.

Upholstery painting

If you think the upholstery or interior panelling of your car requires renovating, or maybe you want to improve the colour scheme or make it look more sporty, there are various colours of upholstery paint available in accessory shops. You can also use the paint to cover up repairs, but make sure it's a perfect match or you could make things look worse.

The Personal Touch

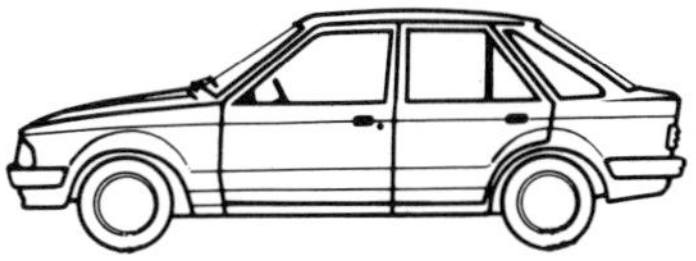

On the subject of accessories it's been said that, if somebody makes it, the motorist will buy it. The 'after-market' in extras and accessories has now grown to enormous proportions, and it can be difficult to sort out the useful and practical items from what, at the other end of the scale, is some undoubted rubbish.

We'd need several volumes to discuss all the various kinds of things you might conceivably buy for your car, and those we have managed to mention can't be gone into in great detail in a book like this. Some time spent browsing around a good motor accessory shop will reveal more than we can here, but nevertheless we hope the suggestions given may prove useful.

All good products will be supplied with general fitting instructions which may or may not require minor modifications to suit your Escort. If you're buying secondhand, of course you may get no instructions at all. The guidelines given here are in no way intended to replace the manufacturer's instructions, and if you're in doubt about fitting a particular item, they're the people to refer to. Don't forget that Ford themselves supply a very wide range of 'tailor made' accessories for all their models.

Note: *always disconnect the battery before commencing any work involving the electrical system. Fireworks are very pretty, but there's a time and place for everything.*

Auxiliary instruments

It would be possible to write a complete book on auxiliary instruments and how to fit them but, as with other things, you'll normally get pretty good instructions when you buy them. Because there are so many instruments available, we're only going to consider battery condition indicators, clocks, oil pressure gauges, tachometers and vacuum gauges.

First of all, even before you've decided what instruments you're going to fit, you've got to think where to fit them. The dash panel of this range of Ford models doesn't lend itself readily to fitting brackets, and small extra panels, because the instruments will end up being rather low down. Some instruments such as tachometers can be pod types, which are attached to the top of the dash panel. Another answer may be a central console, of more exotic type than the standard fitting, which will not only allow you to mount instruments but may have a radio installation compartment and/or a storage pocket. Some information on these is given a little later on.

Sooner or later you're going to have to start drilling some holes somewhere, but this needn't cause any real headaches if it's approached in the right way. As already mentioned, make sure there's nothing behind the panel before even considering drilling a hole, and that there's enough room to fit the instrument, switch, or whatever, in the space chosen. Any hole which will have a cable or capillary running through it must have a plastic or rubber grommet to prevent the metal chafing through; these grommets can be obtained from D-I-Y accessory or car electrical shops.

When it comes to drilling larger holes for instruments, start off by centre-punching the middle of the area, then use compasses or dividers to mark the hole, allowing a little for clearance (standard instruments are 2 in/52 mm diameter). It's best to mark another hole inside the first hole, and drill around this line so that the centre part can readily be pushed out; if you're using a $\frac{1}{8}$ in drill, the inner circle will need to

Some of the supplementary instruments and other accessories available from Smiths Industries

be $\frac{1}{16}$ in inside the first circle marked. Finish the job off by carefully filing and deburring the hole.

An alternative method of cutting large holes is to use a tank cutter of the type used by plumbers. Some of these, which resemble a circular hacksaw blade, can be purchased in a variety of diameters and will fit in an electric drill, so removing much of the hard work.

Battery condition indicator

The battery condition indicator is simply a voltmeter, and as such must be connected to a good earth point on the chassis and to any suitable connection which is live when the ignition switch is 'on'.

Clock

Clocks come in many forms, but most types contain semi-conductors. If this means nothing to you, remember that while it ensures a negligible load on the battery it does mean that the polarity (positive/negative connections) is critical if you don't want to cause permanent damage, so watch the maker's instructions here. Connections are much the same as for the battery condition indicator except that you don't want the clock to stop when the ignition's switched off, so make your connection to a lead or terminal which is live with the ignition switch 'off'.

Tachometer

The tachometer (rev counter) is the one instrument that's available in larger sizes than the others (80 mm instead of 52 mm, although this smaller size can be obtained). Most are positive *or* negative earth, but you must connect them up correctly. In case you should pick up a secondhand one, connections for the most common types are shown in the illustrations. Note that with the Smiths type, the distributor-to-coil LT lead is removed. Use a 14/0.30 (14/0.12) cable size.

Oil pressure gauge

Your Escort won't be equipped with an oil pressure gauge, but only a warning lamp as original equipment. You can install a gauge by first removing the oil pressure switch from the cylinder block and screwing in a T-piece. The switch at the oil gauge pipe can then be connected to the T-piece, so having

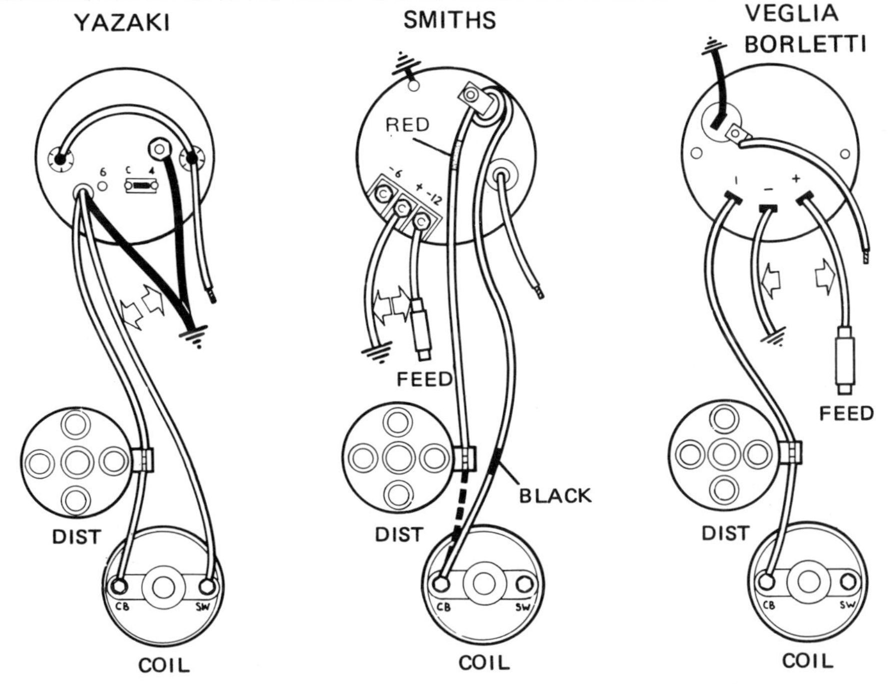

Connections for three popular makes of tachometer

Yazaki: *Negative earth shown – reverse arrowed wires to change polarity*
Smiths: *Positive earth shown – the dotted connection must be removed when the tachometer is fitted. Reverse arrowed wires to change polarity*
Veglia Borletti: *Negative earth shown – reverse arrowed wires to change polarity*

Removing oil pressure switch (CVH engine)

the benefit of a gauge as well as retaining the warning light, which is more likely to be noticed in the event of a sudden oil pressure drop than is the needle on the gauge under normal driving conditions.

Vacuum gauge (performance gauge or fuel consumption gauge)

This is simply a suction (negative pressure) gauge which screws into a tapping on the inlet manifold, with a flexible pipe to the gauge. Once you've got the hang of using it, it can be very useful as an aid to economical driving.

Consoles

Consoles come in all shapes, sizes and prices, and can provide a replacement for the rather basic standard fitting if supplementary instruments, radio cassette player, etc, are to be accommodated. Before buying, have a good look round to see what's on the market – that includes looking through the motoring D-I-Y magazines. Some types extend back from the engine compartment wall or dash panel to behind the handbrake, the handbrake and gear levers coming up through the console base panel. You can get them with cut-outs for switches, radios and tape players, and for the standard 52 mm diameter circular instruments. Many types also have an ashtray or storage pocket; some have an arm-rest; there's even a type that fits to the roof! They come in a variety of finishes – black leatherette, fibreglass, or woodgrain, and in various colours. Without a great deal of difficulty you should be able to get something that suits both your taste and your pocket.

Fitting's usually straightforward, but you may need to drill a few extra holes which could lead to your buying some self-tapping screws as well. Before drilling, don't forget to look on the other side of the panel, or your console could prove rather expensive!

Warning devices

Air horns

Air horns are marketed by several companies as a D-I-Y installation kit comprising the horns themselves, a compressor unit, a relay, plastic piping and-

Fiamm 'Trio' air horns

electrical cable. What you've obviously got to do is mount the horns reasonably near the compressor, and the compressor reasonably near the relay, or the connections just won't reach. It's normal for the manufacturers to specify a certain way up for the compressor to be mounted, but there shouldn't be any other problems. You'll need to make sure that the electrical connections are as per the maker's instructions for the relay and compressor, and decide whether you want to use the air horns in conjunction with, or in place of, the original car horn. If you have to connect into existing wiring, make sure the connections are well made and, if these involve soldering, don't forget to insulate any soldered joints.

Child safety seats and harnesses

Much has been said in recent years about the use of seat belts for front seat passengers, and more recently there's been an increasing interest in the various special rear seats and harnesses now available for young children. It's very difficult to give any precise instructions for fitting these, because there are so many types around, but what you must be careful about is ensuring that you buy a BSI-approved kind.

Most types have a pair of straps at the lower edge which need to be attached to the rear seat pan at the back of the squab, and a further pair of straps that fit over the back of the car seat for attachment to the floor. Take very careful note of the manufacturer's instructions; they require the anchorages to be a certain distance apart, and may also require reinforcing plates to be used. Before starting to drill holes for the mountings, make sure the underside or rear of the panel's clear of obstructions, pipes or any other components, particularly the petrol tank!

Lamps

When auxiliary lamps are fitted, not only must you fit them in a suitable place on the car, but that place must also meet certain legal requirements; where these apply we've attempted to give some guide lines.

In addition to the actual lights themselves, we have to think of the switch (not normally difficult because many small switch panels are available) fusing, cable sizes and whether relays are necessary.

Spot and fog lamps

It's illegal to mount these with the upper edge of the illuminating surface *more* than 1200 mm (47.24 in) from the ground. Any lamps that are mounted with the lower edge of the illuminating surface *less* than 500 mm (19.69 in) above the ground may only be used in fog or falling snow. In these conditions the lamps must always be mounted and used in pairs (two fog, two spot or one of each) if they're to be used independently of the headlamps.

Their outer edges must be *within* 400 mm (15.75 in) of the edge of the car and (in the case of vehicles first used before January 1, 1971 only) their inner edges must be *not less than* 350 mm (13.78 in) apart. If they're used as spotlamps, they should conform to the normal anti-dazzle requirements, eg by wiring them so that they go out when the headlamps are dipped, or by angling them slightly downwards. Where the law requires headlamps to be used, eg at night on an unlit road, a single lamp may be used only *in conjunction with* the headlamps.

Choose the lamps carefully, and if possible match the lamp styles. There are many good types on sale, so if you're not sure what you want ask for advice. The actual mounting is not too difficult; make up or purchase brackets which will bolt to the bodyframe members and pass through the lower radiator air grille slots. Don't bolt lamps directly to the plastic air griller or bumper assembly unless support brackets can be fitted at the rear.

To prevent overloading of the existing wiring, a relay should be used (the Lucas 6RA type, part No 33213, is suitable). This is connected through the switch from the existing headlamp circuit to one of the relay 'coil' terminals, the other going to a good earth point. The lamp wires then go to one of the relay 'contact' terminals, with the other terminal being connected either to the battery or the battery connection at the starter solenoid, via a line fuse. The fuse rating will depend on the lamp manufacturer's recommendations, but will probably be about 20 amps for a pair of lamps.

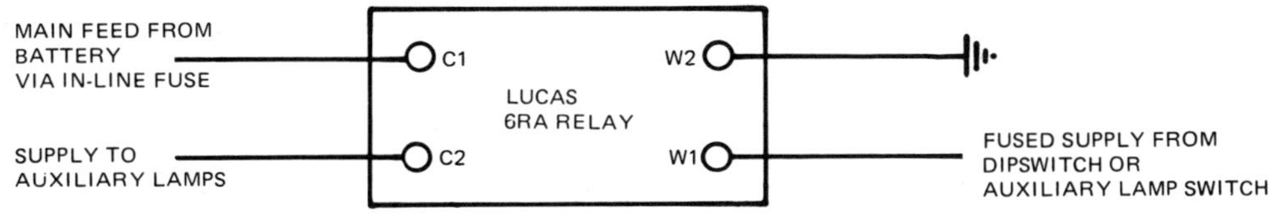

Auxiliary lamp relay connections

Anti-theft devices

There are three main categories of car thieves – those people who want your car either as a compete item or for the major mechanical and body parts; those who are out for a joy-ride; and those who merely want the contents. With any type of thief it makes sense to do what you can to deter someone from *wanting* to get in; don't leave valuables lying about, don't leave the car unlocked and, if it's parked at home, put it in a locked garage if possible. If a car thief decides he does want your particular car, statistically he's got a pretty good chance of getting it!

All Escorts have a steering column lock which is a very effective precaution against a car being driven away, but it still makes sense to have a good burglar alarm fitted. Many types are available, and many of these are wired into door courtesy light switches or hidden switches beneath seats.

Other types are wired into the horn circuit, but separate horns and bells are available; the more unconventional it is (whilst still being reliable!) the better. Don't put hidden switches in the first place you think of – it might be the first place the thief thinks of too.

Some anti-theft devices are activated by the movement caused through trying to get into the car (and occasionally by an innocent passer-by!). Some not only sound alarms, but also earth the ignition circuit; other devices simply mechanically lock together the steering wheel and the brake pedal. Have a look round the accessory shops and see what suits your car, your pocket and the degree of protection required.

Radios and tape players

Nearly all models will be fitted with at least a radio as standard. However, if for some reason you wish to fit a non-standard radio or tape player, this section may provide useful notes.

A radio or tape player is an expensive item to buy, and will only give its best performance if fitted properly. It's useless to expect concert hall performance from a unit that is suspended from the dash panel by string with its speaker resting on the back seat or parcel shelf! If you don't wish to do the installation yourself there are many in-car entertainment specialists who can do the fitting for you.

Make sure the unit purchased is of the same polarity as the car. Ensure that units with adjustable polarity are correctly set before commencing installation.

It's difficult to give specific information with regard to fitting, as final positioning of the radio/tape player, speakers and aerial is entirely a matter of personal preference. However, the following paragraphs give guidelines to follow, which are relevant to all installations.

Radios

Most radios are a standardised size of 7 inches wide, by 2 inches deep – this ensures that they'll fit into the radio aperture provided. If for some reason you are fitting a radio elsewhere, the following points should be borne in mind before deciding exactly where to fit the unit:

(a) The unit must be within easy reach of the driver wearing a seat belt.
(b) The unit mustn't be mounted close to an electric tachometer, the ignition switch and its wiring, or the flasher unit and associated wiring.
(c) The unit must be mounted within reach of the aerial lead, and in such a place that the aerial lead won't have to be routed near the components detailed in paragraph 'b'.
(d) The unit shouldn't be positioned in a place where it might cause injury to the car occupants in an accident; for instance, under the dash panel above the driver's or passenger's legs.
(e) The unit must be fitted really securely.

An aerial is fitted as standard equipment. However, if for some reason you are fitting an aerial elsewhere, bear in mind the following points. The type of aerial used, and where you're going to fit it, is a matter of personal preference. In general, the taller the aerial, the better the reception, but there are limits to what's practicable. If you can, fit a fully retractable type – it saves an awful lot of problems with vandals and car wash equipment. When choosing a suitable spot for an aerial, remember the following points:

(a) The aerial lead should be as short as possible.
(b) The aerial should be mounted as far away from the distributor and HT leads as possible.
(c) The part of the aerial which protrudes beneath the mounting point must not foul the roadwheels, or anything else.
(d) If possible the aerial should be positioned so that the lead does not have to be routed through the engine compartment.
(e) The aerial should be mounted at a more-or-less vertical angle.

Radio interference suppression

Books have been written on the subject, so we're not going to be able to tell you a lot in this small space. To reduce the possibility of your radio picking up unwanted interference, an in-line choke should be

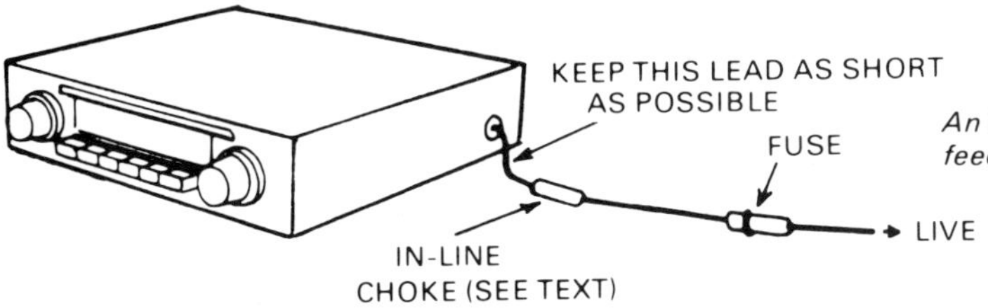

An in-line choke should be fitted in the feed wire as close to the unit as possible

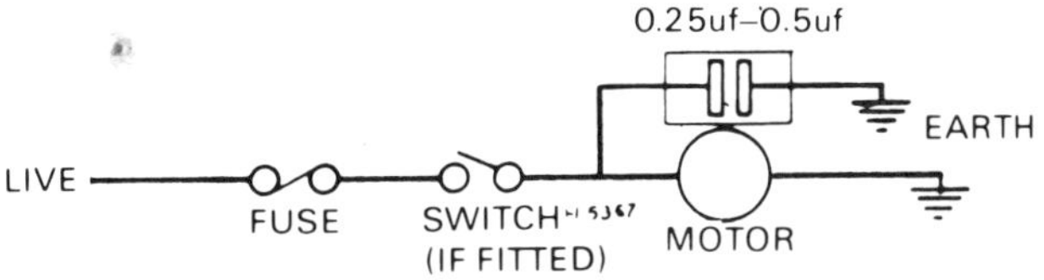

The correct way to suppress electric motors which are causing interference

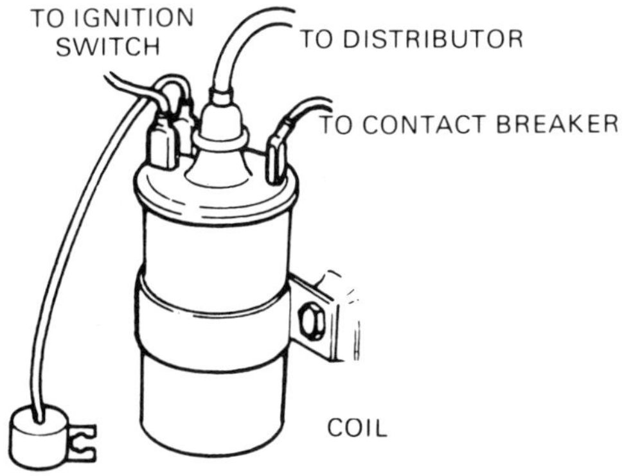

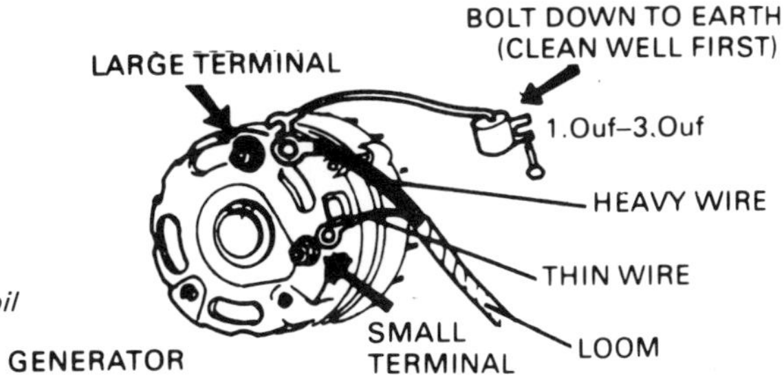

The correct way to connect a capacitor to the coil (above) and the generator (right)

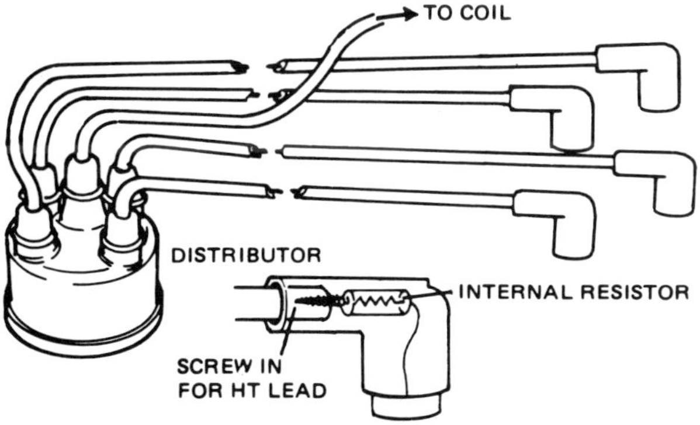

Ignition HT lead suppressors

Left:
Resistive suppressor-type plug caps.

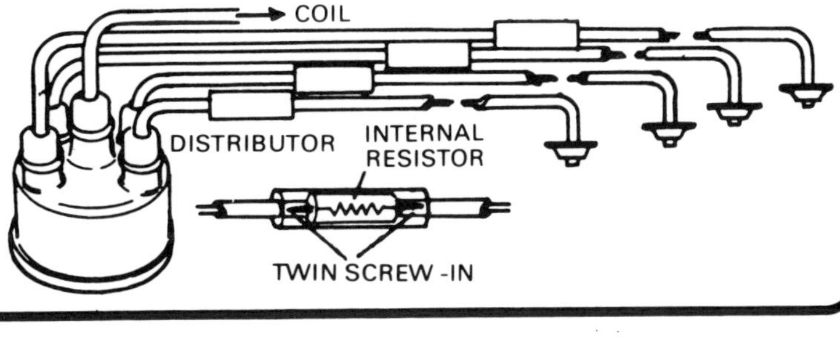

Right:
Resistive in-line suppressors

fitted in the feed wire and the set itself must be earthed really securely.

The next step is to start connecting capacitors to reduce the amount of interference being generated by the different circuits of the car's electrics. The accompanying illustrations show the various interference generators and give capacitor values for the suppressors.

When it comes to the ignition HT leads, these are resistors which can either be suppressor-type plug caps or in-line suppressors; if you're already using resistive HT leads (those with the carbon fibre filling), they're already doing the job for you. On some models, the windscreen wiper motor can cause interference. Try earthing the wiper motor bracket to the body to cure it.

Tape players

Fitting instructions for both cartridge and cassette stereo players are the same and in general the same rules apply as when fitting a radio. Tape players aren't usually prone to electrical interference like radios – although it can occur – so positioning isn't so critical. If possible the player should be mounted on an even keel. Also, it must be possible for a driver wearing a seat belt to reach the unit in order to change or turn over tapes.

Comfort

Longer journeys can be much more pleasant if your car's comfortable to drive, and just a couple of suggestions on this theme may be welcome.

Sound reducing kits

Very few cars have yet been produced in which the noise level, particularly at motorway speeds, is all that could be desired. For economy reasons, most manufacturers put only a certain amount of underfelt and sound-deadening material into their cars, and a further improvement can usually be made by fitting one of the proprietary kits. These are usually tailored to fit individual models, and consist of sections of felt-like material which are glued in place under carpets, inside hollow sections, boot lid etc, in accordance with instructions. The material can also be bought in rolls for D-I-Y cutting, using the carpets etc as templates.

Seats

If your car seats are showing signs of old age (and fitting new covers won't disguise the sagging when you sit in them) then you can of course have them rebuilt by an upholstery specialist. On the other hand, you could think about replacing at least the driver's seat by one of the special bucket types available. To look at these you'll have to find an

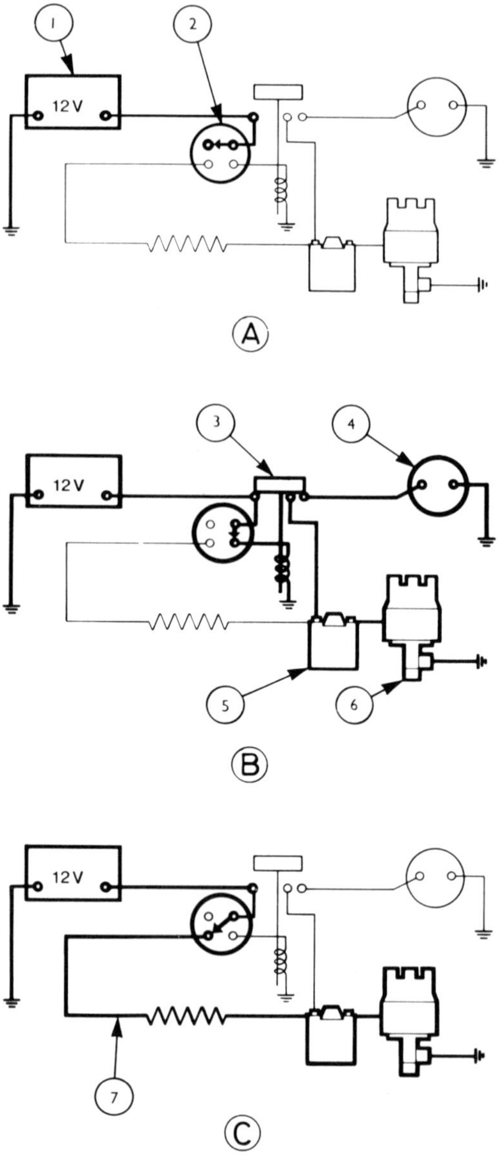

Ignition circuit (ohv models) showing action of ballast resistor

- *A* *Ignition switch off (O)*
- *B* *Ignition switch in START position (III)*
- *C* *Ignition switch in normal running position (II)*
- *1* *Battery*
- *2* *Ignition switch*
- *3* *Starter solenoid*
- *4* *Starter motor*
- *5* *Ignition coil*
- *6* *Distributor*
- *7* *Ballast resistor*

accessory shop stocking the more motor sport orientated kind of goods.

Miscellaneous

Electronic ignition

Owners of 1.1 engined Escorts may consider converting the mechanical contact breaker type ignition system to an electronic one. Larger engined versions have electronic ignition fitted as standard.

Such systems are many and varied and widely advertised. The makers claim easier starting, better performance and lower fuel consumption as the main advantages, and sometimes marginal improvements are obtained.

However, before buying one of the available kits we suggest you stop and reflect whether your mileage and type of driving makes the expenditure worthwhile. Get other advice, preferably from someone who's fitted such a system to his own car. Consider too whether you're capable of installing it yourself, otherwise you'll have to pay for fitting as well.

If you decide to install electronic ignition, buy a system that will enable you to dispose of your mechanical contact breaker set (some systems still retain them). Then at least you can save money on the purchase of contact sets and time on the routine servicing of the contact breaker points.

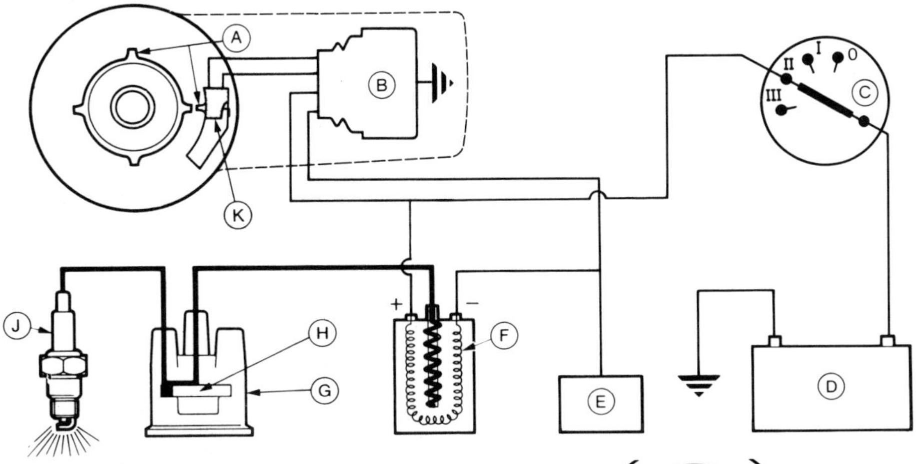

A Trigger wheel
B Module (switched off)
C Ignition key (in position II)
D Battery
E Tachometer
F Coil primary circuit cut with resultant HT voltage
G Distributor cap
H Rotor arm
J Spark plug
K Coil with no current flow (change-over point)

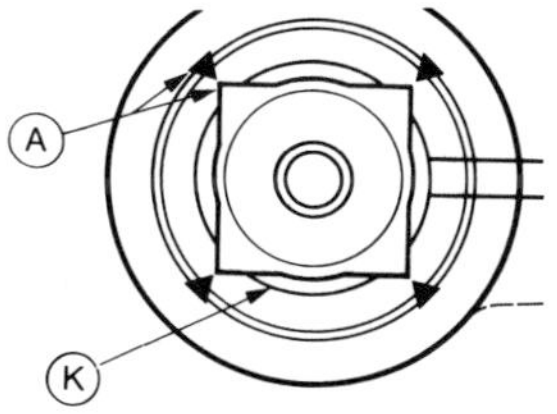

A Trigger switch
K Coil with no current flow (change-over point)

Lucas breakerless ignition circuit shown at firing point (CVH models)

Bosch distributor shown inset

Steering wheels

One of the more popular, easily fitted accessories is a special steering wheel. Many types are available, but often it's also necessary to buy a boss which fits on to the steering column shaft, to which the steering wheel is then attached. No problems should be encountered when fitting a steering wheel or boss, once the old steering wheel has been taken off.

To remove the wheel, first disconnect the battery and then set the front roadwheels in the straight-ahead position.

According to model, either pull off the steering wheel trim or prise out the insert which carries the Ford motif at the centre of the steering wheel. Hold the steering wheel from turning while the steering wheel retaining nut is unscrewed using a socket with extension. Remove the steering wheel from the shaft. No effort should be required to remove the steering wheel, as it is located on a hexagonal section shaft which does not cause the binding associated with splined shafts. Note the steering shaft direction indicator cam which has its peg uppermost.

When installing the new wheel, check that the roadwheels are in the straight-ahead attitude so that the steering wheel spokes can be positioned to suit normal straight-ahead driving. Tighten the steering wheel retaining nut securely. If you have a torque wrench, the nut should be tightened to 24 lbf ft (32 Nm). If you haven't a torque wrench, ask your dealer to check the tightness next time you call in.

Removing steering wheel trim

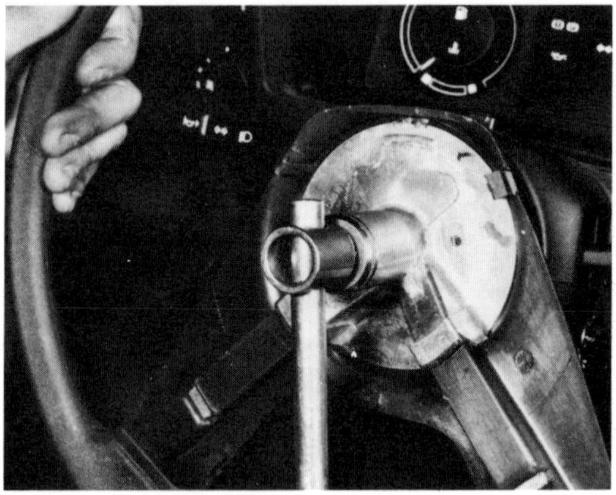

Unscrewing steering wheel retaining nut

Steering wheel removed

Roof racks

The types available are very varied, but they normally rely on clips attached to the water drain channel above the doors. If you're buying, select a size that suits your requirements, making sure that it's not too wide for the roof!

When fitting the roof rack, position it squarely on the roof, preferably towards the front rather than the rear. After it's loaded, by the way, recheck the tension of the attachment bracket screws.

Don't keep the roof rack on when it's not wanted; it offers too much wind resistance, creates a surprising amount of noise and makes your fuel economy suffer.

Dog/luggage guards

Many dog owners or those who carry large loads in the rear of the vehicle will no doubt find one of these tubular barriers a boon. They're normally adjustable telescopically, both for height and width, and are fitted by clamping between roof and load deck immediately behind the rear seat to keep dog, luggage or whatever in its rightful place, and possibly prevent injury to the front seat occupants in an emergency stop.

MAG Universal dog guard

Mudflaps

You're probably already aware that both front and rear wheel arches can be fitted with mudflaps. These will not only protect your car's underside and paintwork from flying stones, but will also earn the thanks of following drivers owing to the reduction in spray during wet weather. Fitting's straightforward and is usually by means of clamping brackets or self-tapping screws.

Specialist fitments

We've now covered a lot of main items likely to interest the average owner from the D-I-Y fitting angle. Such things as towbars and sunshine or vinyl roofs, while practical or desirable, are beyond the scope of both this book and of the ordinary car owner. We therefore recommend that for any major accessory of this kind you consult the appropriate specialist who'll be able to give you an initial estimate of the cost as well as carrying out the work properly and safely.

Troubleshooting

We've gone to great lengths in this book to provide as much information on your car as we think you'll need for satisfactory running and servicing. Hopefully, you won't need to use this section but there's always a possibility (rather than a probability!) that something will go wrong, and by reference to the charts that follow you should be able to pinpoint the trouble even if you can't actually fix it yourself.

The charts are broken down into the main systems of the car, and where there's a fairly straightforward remedy – the sort you can tackle yourself – **bold type** is used to highlight it. Further information on that particular item will normally be found elsewhere in the book; look up the particular component or system in the index to find the correct page. In some cases a reference number will be found (eg T1/1); by looking up this number in the accompanying cross-reference table, you'll find more information on that particular fault.

When confronted with a fault, try to think calmly and logically about the symptom(s), and you'll soon be able to work out what the fault *can't* be! Check or substitute one item at a time, otherwise when you do clear the fault you may not know exactly what was causing it. The commonest cause of difficulty in starting, especially in winter, is poor spark at the plugs combined with a slow cranking speed from the starter motor. Make sure that your battery's kept fully charged, that the HT leads, coil and distributor cap are clean and dry, that the contact breaker points (1.1 engines only) are in good condition and correctly gapped, and that all connections are clean and tight. If all this is in order, then proceed with fault finding in other areas.

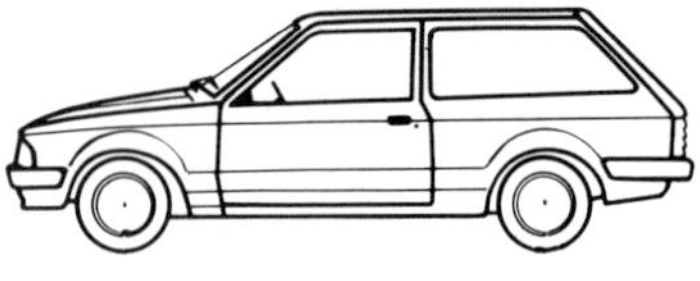

CROSS-REFERENCE TABLE

TROUBLESHOOTER REFERENCE	ADDITIONAL INFORMATION
T1/1	Either charge the battery from a battery charger, or use jump leads to start the car from another battery, make sure that the lead polarities are correct in both cases or you may do permanent damage.
T1/2	If the lead's loose, disconnect the battery earth lead then tighten the connection on the starter motor. Reconnect the battery earth lead.
T1/3	Select 3rd gear and have a friend give you a push. As soon as you gather speed, let in the clutch. Drive to your dealer for (possibly) a new starter motor.
T1/4	Make sure all the connections are tight, then wipe the leads clean and dry with a lint-free cloth. Use an ignition system waterproofer (eg WD40 or Damp Start) to prevent it happening again if this is a regular problem with your car.
T1/5	An ignition coil or condenser is a simple item to fit, but make a note of the connections before removing them, and ensure that the replacement coil is the correct type for mechanical or electronic ignition.
T1/6	To check the operation of the pump, detach the fuel outlet pipe (that's the one that goes to the carburettor) and operate it by turning the engine over on the starter a few times. There should be a steady stream of petrol in spurts if the pump's working properly. Take care you don't spill fuel on the hot exhaust! Cleaning the fuel pump gauze filter is covered in the 6000 mile Service Schedule.
T1/7	It's easy enough to tighten the attachment bolts if you've got a box or socket spanner of the right size.
T1/8	For a temporary repair a leaking water hose can normally be bound up with adhesive tape or, better still, with a hose bandage specially made for this purpose.
T1/9	Wait till the system's cooled down, then top it up. If it happens a second time, get it looked at straight away or you could ruin your engine (if it hasn't happened already). If it's just a leaking water hose you can probably bind it up as in T1/8 (above) to get yourself home.
T2/1	Driving carefully will probably get you home. An air line on the radiator core will clean out the dirt that's accumulated; it it's blocked internally, use a proprietary flushing compound.
T2/2	You may be able to repair the hose temporarily, as in T1/8, but it'll almost certainly mean a new one as soon as possible.
T2/3	Drive slower and don't labour the engine.
T4/1	You'll need a little extra pedal effort for braking but that's all. It may be possible to temporarily repair the vacuum hose as in T1/8.
T6/1	Remove the lamp lenses (see *In an Emergency)* and check for signs of rust. Where there's rust, scrape it off and apply a little petroleum jelly. Ensure that the screws securing the lamp body to the car are making good contact.

TROUBLESHOOTER 1:

Starter motor doesn't work when key is turned (no noise from motor)

- Battery problem
  - **Flat battery (T1/1). Battery connections loose or corroded.** Battery defective
- Other causes
  - Starter motor or solenoid switch faulty internally. **Loose connection to starter (T1/2)**

Starter motor doesn't work properly

- Turns engine very slowly
  - **Battery flat (T1/1) or defective.** Internal starter motor fault. **Loose connection to starter (T1/2).** Starter motor brushes badly worn or sticking. **Battery connections loose or corroded**

Spark plug lead(s) loose, disconnected, damp or faulty (T1/4). Spark plugs dirty, cracked or incorrectly gapped. Distributor or coil cap damp, cracked or HT lead loose. Worn distributor cap electrodes. Coil or condenser faulty (T1/5). Contact breaker points dirty or incorrectly set (ohv only). Ignition timing incorrect

ENGINE – STARTING

Starting motor turns engine normally but engine won't start

Doesn't turn engine (Just whirrs or clicks)

Works noisily or harshly

Ignition system fault

Other causes

Starter pinion teeth stripped.
Starter internal fault

Starter motor retaining bolts loose (T1/7)

Fuel system fault

Air cleaner clogged.
Valve clearances incorrect (ohv only).
Inlet manifold or gasket, or carburettor gasket leaking.
Brake servo hose leaking (T4/1).
Engine seriously overheated (T1/9)

Pinion or flywheel teeth broken or worn

Fuel pump faulty or **filter blocked (T1/6).**
Fuel tank empty.
Leak in fuel pump or fuel lines.
Carburettor jets blocked.
Fuel lines blocked.
Carburettor float chamber fuel level incorrect.
Carburettor incorrectly adjusted.
Choke not operating correctly

TROUBLESHOOTER 2:

Lacks power

Ignition fault

Spark plugs dirty or incorrectly gap-ped.
Contact breaker points dirty or in-correctly set (ohv only).
Ignition timing in-correct.
Distributor, vacuum unit or connecting hose faulty

Fuel system fault

Other causes

Incorrect valve clearances (ohv only).
Low cylinder com-pression.
Air cleaner clog-ged.
Blown cylinder head gasket

Other causes

Cracked cylind
block or head.
Valves or valve
seats badly pitt

Overheating

Insufficient water in cooling sys-tem/leakage from system (T1/9).
Drive belt slipping (ohv).
Radiator blocked or grille obstructed (T2/1).
Water hose col-lapsed or kinked (T2/2).
Thermostat not op-erating properly.
Exhaust system obstructed or damaged.
Blown cylinder head gasket.
Engine not yet run-in (T2/3).
Brakes binding.
Oil level too low.
Ignition timing in-correct.
Cracked cylinder block or head.
Electric cooling fan faulty or **fuse blown**

ENGINE – RUNNING

- Misfires
  - Ignition fault
    - **Spark plug lead(s) loose, disconnected, damp or faulty (T1/4).**
    - **Spark plugs dirty, cracked or incorrectly gapped.**
    - **Distributor or coil cap damp, cracked or HT lead loose.**
    - **Worn distributor cap electrodes.**
    - **Coil or condenser faulty (T1/5).**
    - **Contact breaker points dirty or incorrectly set (ohv only).**
    - **Ignition timing incorrect**
  - Fuel system fault
    - Fuel pump faulty or **filter blocked (T1/6).**
    - Leak in fuel pump or fuel lines.
    - Carburettor jet blocked.
    - Carburettor float chamber fuel level incorrect.
    - Carburettor incorrectly adjusted.
    - Choke not operating correctly.
- Cuts out unexpectedly
  - Ignition fault.
    - **Water on ignition components (T1/4).**
    - **Coil or condenser faulty (T1/5).**
    - **LT lead to coil or distributor disconnected (T1/4).**
    - **HT lead from coil loose or disconnected (T1/4).**
  - Fuel system fault
    - **Tank empty.**
    - Fuel pump faulty or **filter blocked (T1/6).**
    - Leak in fuel pump or fuel lines.
    - Carburettor jet blocked.
    - Fuel lines blocked

TROUBLESHOOTER 3:

- Judder/vibration
  - On letting in clutch
    - Engine/transmission mountings loose or perished.
      Clutch friction surfaces badly worn or oily.
      Release mechanism worn.
      Driveshaft constant velocity joints worn
  - When running
    - Steering or suspension fault (Troubleshooter 5)
    - Final drive worn.
      Low oil level in transmission or of incorrect grade.
      Driveshaft constant velocity joints worn
- Gearchange problems
  - Difficulty in engaging or changing gear
    - Synchromesh mechanism worn or damaged.
      Clutch adjustment incorrect.
      Clutch cable frayed or partially seized
  - Jumping out of gear
    - Gearchange selector mechanism worn or damaged

CLUTCH, GEARBOX AND FINAL DRIVE

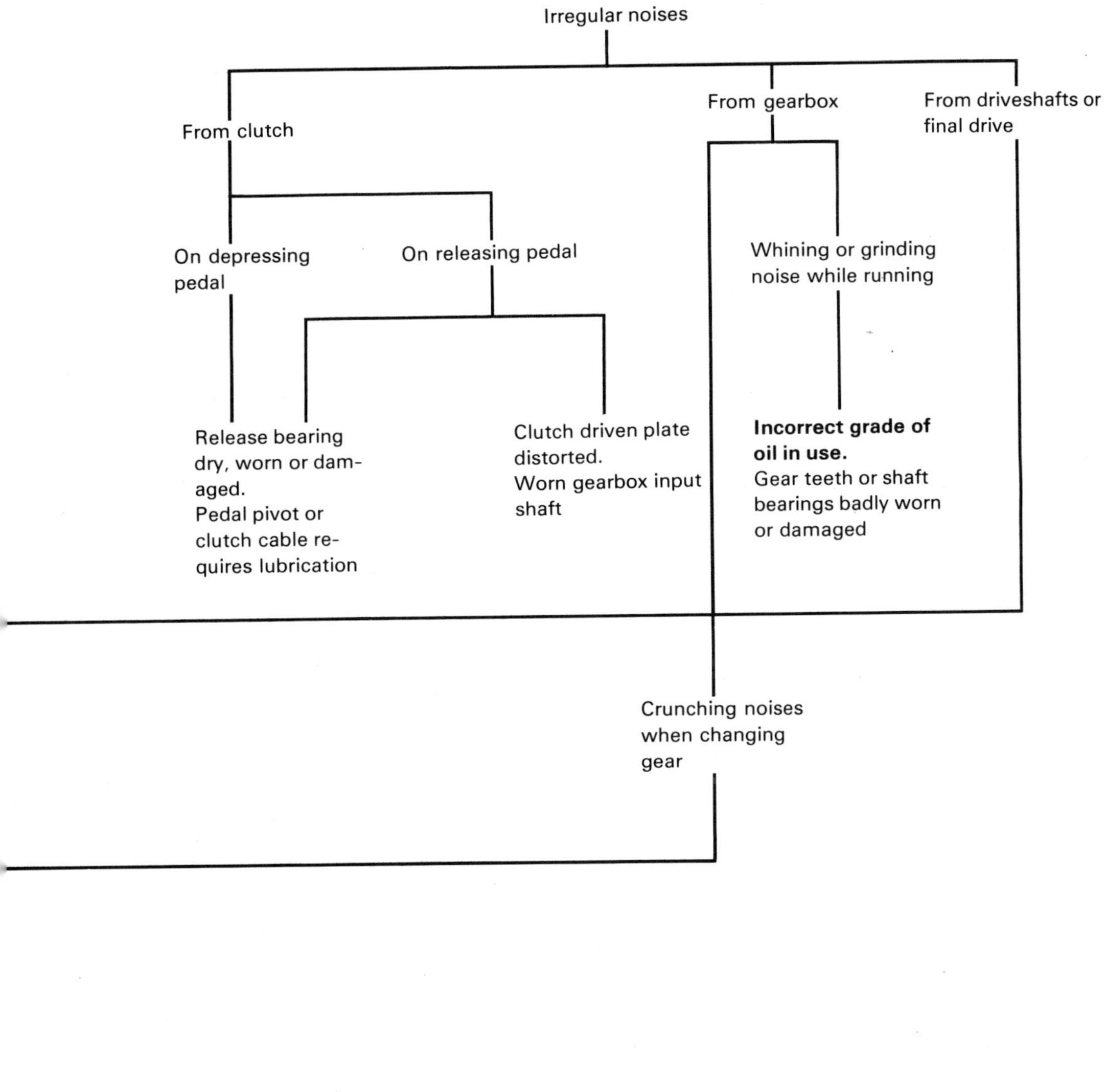

TROUBLESHOOTER 4:

Pedal operation

- Excessive pedal travel
  - **Fluid level too low.** Rear brake self-adjusting mechanism faulty
  - Leaks in system
    - Wheel cylinder or caliper leaking. Master cylinder leaking. Brake line or hose leaking
- 'Spongy' feel
  - Leaks in system
  - Air in system (requires bleeding)
- 'Springy' feel or high pedal pressure needed
  - New linings/pads not yet bedded in. Drums/discs badly scored or distorted. Master cylinder bolts loose. Linings contaminated by dirt, oil, grease or fluid. **Brake servo faulty or hose loose or damaged (T4/1)**

TROUBLESHOOTER 5:

- Steering feels light and vague
  - **Tyre pressures too high. Wrong type of tyre being used**
  - Suspension geometry or tracking wrong. Bodyframe distorted
  - Steering balljoints or swivels badly worn. Steering gear needs adjusting. Steering column coupling loose
- Steering wheel has too much free play
  - Steering balljoints or swivels badly worn. Steering gear needs adjusting. Steering column coupling loose
- Steering feels stiff and heavy
  - **Tyre pressures too low.** Suspension geometry wrong. Steering gear incorrectly adjusted. Steering column badly distorted. Steering rack in need of lubrication

BRAKES

Effect on car

Car pulls to one side

Tyre pressures unequal.
Drums/linings or pads/discs contaminated with oil, grease or fluid.
Brake backplate, caliper or disc loose.
Shoes or pads incorrectly fitted.
Differing types of linings fitted at each side.
Suspension anchorages loose.
Drums/discs badly worn or distorted

Brakes 'grab' or wheel(s) lock

Contamination by dirt, oil, grease or fluid

Brakes bind when pedal released

Handbrake over-adjusted.
Master cylinder pushrod out of adjustment.
Vent hole in reservoir cap blocked.
Master cylinder or wheel cylinder seized.
Faulty automatic adjusters on rear brakes

STEERING/SUSPENSION

Wobble/vibration from front wheels

Loose roadwheel bolts.
Damaged wheel.
Wheels/tyres need balancing.
Steering/suspension ball-joints worn.
Hub bearings worn

Car settles too low or leans to one side while stationary

Weak or broken springs

Car leans over excessively when cornering

Weak or broken springs.
Worn shock absorbers.
Low tyre pressures.
Anti-roll bar (1.3 and 1.6 models only) cracked or mountings loose

TROUBLESHOOTER 6:

NOTE: This chart assumes that the battery installed in your car is in good condition and is of the correct specification, and that the terminal connections are clean and tight. A car used frequently for stop-start motoring or for short journeys (particularly in winter when lights, heater blower etc are likely to be in use) may need its battery recharged at intervals to keep it serviceable. If an electrical problem occurs, don't immediately suspect the starter or any other component without first checking that the battery is capable of supplying its demands.

Fuel gauge

- Gives no reading
  - **Tank empty!** Cable between tank unit and gauge broken or disconnected. Gauge defective
  - Cable or connection loose, broken, corroded or disconnected. **Fuse blown**
- Registers 'Full' all the time.
  - Cable between tank unit and gauge earthed

Horn

- Works all the time
  - Horn push earthed or stuck down. Cable from horn to horn push earthed
- Doesn't work
  - Cable or connection loose, broken, corroded or disconnected. **Fuse blown**

A fault occurring in any other electrical equipment or accessory not specifically referred to can usually be traced to one of the three main causes, ie blown fuse; loose or broken connection to power supply or earth; or internal fault in the component concerned.

ELECTRICS

- Lights
  - Don't come on OR come on but then go out
    - **Battery flat (T1/1).**
      Bulb or filament broken.
      Light switch faulty
  - Work erratically or flicker on and off
    - Light switch faulty
    - **Lamps not earthing properly or corroded (T6/1)**
  - Give very poor light
    - **Lamps not earthing properly or corroded (T6/1)**
    - **Bulbs or lenses dirty or reflectors dirty or corroded.**
      Wrong bulbs installed
- Charging circuit
  - Battery discharges but ignition light works normally
    - Battery defective or **electrolyte low.**
      Battery terminals loose or corroded
    - Generator not charging properly.
      Short-circuit in electrical system.
      Drivebelt slipping
  - Battery discharges and ignition light fails to go out
    - **Drivebelt broken or slipping.**
      Generator brushes worn or sticking
    - Generator internal fault, probably in regulator diode assembly

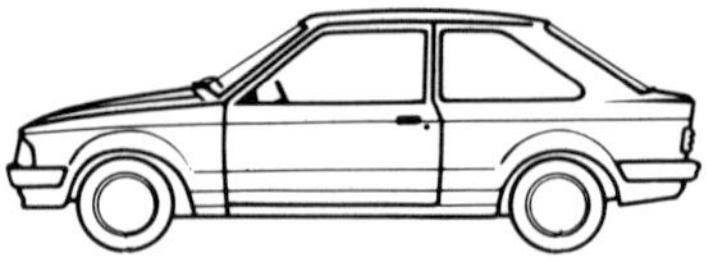

Car Jargon Explained

We hope there isn't much in this Handbook that you can't understand. However, most of us – particularly if we're trying to learn more about an unfamiliar subject – will sooner or later come across the odd word or phrase that needs explaining. This alphabetical list should help you understand the language spoken by your garage man, 'expert' neighbour, or that inevitable chap in the local...

A

Accelerator pump: A device attached to many *carburettors* which adds a spurt of extra fuel to the carburettor mixture when the accelerator pedal is suddenly pressed down.

Additives: Compounds which are added to petrol and lubricating oil to improve their quality and performance.

Advance and retard: A system for altering the ignition timing – the time in the firing cycle at which the ignition spark occurs. The spark timing is normally a few degrees of *crankshaft* revolution before the *piston* reaches the top of its stroke, and is expressed as so many degrees before top-dead-centre (BTDC). It's altered by devices in the *distributor* which detect changes in engine speed and load. Broadly speaking, as the engine speeds up the ignition is advanced (greater angle BTDC) but if there is a heavy engine load the ignition is retarded (smaller angle BTDC).

AF: An abbreviation of 'across flats', the way in which many nuts, bolt heads and spanners are now identified. It's preceded by an Imperial or metric unit of measurement – e.g. $\frac{1}{2}$ in AF or 11mm AF.

Air cooling: Alternative method of engine cooling in which no water is used. An engine-driven fan forces air at high velocity over the engine surfaces, which are enclosed by cowling. Normally an *oil cooler* is incorporated in the air flow to assist the rate of heat loss.

Alternator: A device for converting rotating mechanical energy into electrical energy. In modern cars, it has superseded the *dynamo* for charging the battery because of its much greater efficiency.

Ammeter: A device for measuring the current supplied to the battery from the *dynamo* or *alternator,* or drawn from the battery by the car lights, wipers, radio etc.

Antifreeze: A chemical compound mixed with the cooling system water to lower the temperature at which the coolant freezes.

Anti-roll bar: A spring-steel bar mounted transversely across a car which counteracts the natural tendency for the car to lean over when cornering.

Aquaplaning: A phrase used to describe the action of a tyre skating across water.

Automatic transmission: A type of *gearbox* which selects the correct gear ratio automatically according to the engine speed and load.

B

Balljoint: A ball-and-socket type joint, used in steering and *suspension* systems, which permits relative movement in more than one plane.

Battery condition indicator: A voltmeter connected via the ignition switch to the car battery. Unlike an *ammeter* (which it's tending to supersede), it will warn you of impending battery failure.

Bearing: Metal or other hard wearing surface against which another part moves or rotates, and which is designed (and usually lubricated) to withstand the resulting friction.
Bendix drive: A device on many types of starter motor which allows the motor to be coupled to the *flywheel* for engine starting, then disengages when the engine commences to run.
BPH: See *Horsepower.*
Big end: The end of a *connecting rod* which is attached to the *crankshaft.* It incorporates a *bearing* and transmits the linear movement of the con-rod to the motion of the crankshaft.
Bleed nipple (or valve): A hollow screw with a tapered seat which allows air or fluid to be bled out of a system when it is loosened.
Brake caliper: That part of a *disc brake* system which houses the *brake pads* and the *hydraulic* operating pistons.
Brake fade: A temporary loss of braking efficiency due to overheating of the brake friction material.
Brake pad: That part of a *disc brake* system which comprises the friction material and a metal backing plate.
Brake shoe: That part of a *drum brake* system which comprises the friction material and a curved metal former.
Breather: A device which allows fresh air into a system or allows contaminated air out.
Bucket tappet: A cup (or bucket) shaped piece of metal used in some engines to transmit the rotary *camshaft* movement to an up-and-down movement for *valve* operation.
Bump stop: A hard rubber device used in many *suspension* systems to prevent the moving parts from lifting the bodyframe during violent suspension movements.

C

Camber angle: The angle at which the front wheels are set from the vertical, when viewed from the front of the car. Positive camber is the amount in degrees by which the wheels are tilted outwards at the top.
Cam follower: A cylindrical piece of metal used to transmit the rotary *camshaft* movement to an up-and-down movement for *valve* operation.
Camshaft: A rotating shaft with lobes or cams used to operate the engine *valves.*
Carbon fibre leads: Black, string-like cores in the centre of some plug *HT* leads, which don't need separate radio and *TV suppressors.*
Carburettor: A device which is used to mix air and fuel in the correct proportions for all conditions of engine running. There are two main types: those with a number of fixed *jets,* and those with a single jet with a moving needle in it. In the former type, the different jets come into operation at different conditions of throttle opening, engine speed and engine load; in the latter type, the *needle jet* is controlled by a moving *piston,* the position of which depends on the amount of suction in the engine *manifold.*
Castor angle: The angle between the front wheel pivot points and a vertical line when viewed from the side of the car. Positive castor is when the axis is inclined rearwards.
Centrifugal advance: System of ignition *advance and retard* incorporated in many *distributors* in which weights rotating on a shaft alter the ignition timing according to engine speed.
Choke: This has two common meanings. It is used to describe the device which shuts off some of the air in a *carburettor* during cold starting, and may be either manually or automatically operated. It's also used as a general term to describe the carburettor throttle bore.
Clutch: A friction device which allows two rotating devices to be coupled together smoothly, without the need for either rotating part to stop.
Coil spring: A spiral of spring steel used in many *suspension* systems.
Combustion chamber: Shaped area in the *cylinder head* into which the fuel/air mixture is compressed by the *piston* and in which combustion of the mixture is effected by the *spark plug.*
Compression ratio (CR): A term used to describe the amount by which the fuel/air mixture is compressed, and expressed as a number. For example, an 8.5 : 1 compression ratio means that the volume of fuel/air when the *piston* is at the bottom of its stroke is 8.5 times that when the piston is at the top of its stroke.
Compression tester: A special type of pressure gauge screwed into the *spark plug* hole which shows the *cylinder* compression when the engine is turning but not firing.
Condenser (capacitor): A device in the *distributor* which stores electrical energy and prevents excessive sparking at the *contact breaker* points.
Connecting rod (con-rod): Rod in the engine connecting the *piston* to the *crankshaft.*
Constant velocity (CV) joint: A joint used in *driveshafts,* where the speed of the input shaft is exactly the same as the speed of the output shaft at any angle of rotation. This does not occur in ordinary *universal joints.*
Contact breaker: The device in the *distributor* which comprises the electrical points (or contacts),and a cam which opens and closes them to operate the *HT*

electrical circuit which provides the spark at the *spark plug*.

Crossflow cylinder head: A *cylinder head* in which the inlet and exhaust *manifolds* are on opposite sides.

Crossply tyre: A tyre whose construction is such that the weave of the fabric material layers is running diagonally in alternately opposite directions to a line around the circumference.

Cubic capacity: The total volume within the *cylinders* which is swept by the *pistons.*

CVH: A term applied by the Ford Motor Company to their *OHC* engines which incorporate a hemispherical *combustion chamber. CVH* means Compound Valve angle, Hemispherical combustion chamber.

Cylinder head: That part of the engine which contains the *valves* and associated operating gear.

D

Damper: See *shock absorber.*

Dashpot: An oil-filled *cylinder* and *piston* used as a damping device in SU and Zenith/Stromberg CD type *carburettors.*

Dead axle (beam axle): The simplest form of axle, comprising a horizontal member attached to the chassis-frame by springs. This is used for the rear axle on some front-wheel-drive cars.

Decarbonizing ('decoking'): Removal of all carbon deposits from the *combustion chambers* of an engine.

De Dion axle: A rear axle comprising a cranked tube attached to the wheel hubs, with a separately mounted *differential* gear and *driveshafts. Suspension* is normally through *coil springs* between the wheel hubs and chassis frame.

Diaphragm: A stationary flexible membrane used in items such as fuel pumps The diaphragm spring used in clutches is somewhat similar but is made from spring steel.

Diesel engine: An engine which relies upon the heat generated when compressing air to ignite the fuel, and which therefore doesn't need a *spark plug.* Diesel engines have much higher *compression ratios* than petrol engines, normally in the region of 20:1.

Differential: A system of gears (generally known as a crownwheel and pinion) which allows the *torque* from the *propeller shaft* to be applied to the driving wheels. The torque is divided proportionately between the driving wheels to permit one wheel to turn faster than the other if required, for example during cornering.

Din: This stands for Deutsche Industrie Norm (roughly equivalent to the British Standards Institution) and lays down international standards for measuring output, performance, etc., of motor vehicles.

Disc brake: A braking system where a rotating disc is clamped between hydraulically operated friction pads.

Distributor: A collective term used to describe the *contact breaker, advance and retard* mechanisms, and associated parts of the *ignition system.*

Doughnut: A term used to describe the flexible rubber coupling used in some *driveshafts.*

Driveshaft: Name usually applied to the shaft (normally incorporating *universal* or *constant velocity joints)* which transmits the drive from a *transaxle* to one wheel; more commonly found in front-wheel-drive cars.

Drive train: A collective term used to describe the *gearbox, propeller shaft, final drive* and *half-shafts* of a front engine/rear wheel drive car.

Drum brake: A brake with friction linings on 'shoes', running inside a cylindrical drum attached to the wheel.

Dual circuit brakes: A *hydraulic* braking system comprising two separate fluid circuits, so that if one circuit becomes inoperative, braking power is still available from the other circuit at a reduced efficiency.

Dwell angle: The number of degrees of *distributor* cam rotation during which the *contact breaker* points are closed during the ignition cycle of one *cylinder.* The angle is altered by adjusting the points gap, and is a more accurate way of setting-up the *ignition system.*

Dynamo: A device for converting rotating mechanical energy into electrical energy. This is a heavier, less efficient form of *generator* than the *alternator* and has largely been superseded by it during recent years.

E

Earth strap: A flexible electrical connection between the battery and vehicle earth, or the engine/*gearbox* and chassis frame, to provide the return current-flow path in the electrical system.

Electrode: An electrical terminal or terminals, across which a spark occurs e.g., in a *spark plug* or *distributor* cap.

Electrolyte: A current-conducting solution of water and sulphuric acid, which is the liquid inside the car battery.

Electronic ignition: An *ignition system* incorporating electronic components which can produce a much greater spark voltage than in conventional systems.

Emission control: The prevention or reduction of the emission into the atmosphere of noxious fumes and gases from the engine and fuel tank of a motor vehicle. Required to varying degrees by the laws of different countries, it is effected by design and by special devices.

Epicyclic gears (planetary gears): A gear system used in many *automatic transmissions* where there is a centre 'sun' wheel around which smaller 'planet' gears inside a 'planet carrier' rotate.
Exhaust gas analyser: An instrument used for the measurement of pollutants (mainly carbon monoxide) in an exhaust system.
Expansion tank: A container used in many modern cooling systems to collect the overflow from the car's *radiator* as the coolant heats up and expands.

F

Filter: A device for extracting foreign particles from air or oil.
Final drive: A collective term (often expressed as a gearing ratio) for the crownwheel and pinion (see *Differential).*
Flat engine: Form of engine design in which the *cylinders* are positioned horizontally, usually with an equal number each side of a central *crankshaft.*
Float chamber: That part of a *carburettor* which contains a float and *needle valve* for controlling the fuel level.
Flywheel: A heavy rotating disc attached to the *crankshaft* used to smooth out the pulsating output from the *cylinders.*
Four stroke (cycle): A common term used to describe the four operating strokes of a *piston* in a conventional car engine. These are: (1) Induction - drawing in the fuel/air mixture as the piston goes down; (2) Compression of the fuel/air mixture as the piston rises; (3) Power stroke where the piston is forced down after the fuel/air mixture has been ignited by the *spark plug* and (4) Exhaust stroke where the piston rises and pushes the burnt gases out of the *cylinder.* During these operations, the inlet and exhaust *valves* are opened and closed at the correct moment to allow the fuel/air mixture in, the exhaust gases out, or to provide a gas-tight compression chamber.
Fuel injection: A method of injecting fuel into an engine. Used in *Diesel* engines, and also on some petrol engines as a replacement for the *carburettor.*

G

Gasket: Compressible material used between two metal surfaces to make a leakproof joint.
Gearbox: A group of gears and shafts installed in a metal housing. Physically, this is positioned between the *clutch* and the *differential,* and is used to multiply the engine *torque.*
Generator: See *alternator* and *dynamo.*

H

Half-shaft: A rotating shaft, two of which are used to transmit the drive from the *differential* to the wheels.
Hardy-Spicer joint (Hooke's or Cardan joint): See *Universal joint.*
Helical gears: Gears in which the teeth are cut at a slant across the circumference to give smoother meshing and quieter running.
Horsepower: A measurement of the rate of doing work. Where brake horsepower *(BPH)* is referred to, it's the amount of work required to stop a moving body.
HT: Abbreviation of high tension (meaning high voltage). Used in connection with the ignition system.
Hydraulic: A term used to describe the operation of a system by means of fluid pressure.

I

Ignition system: The electrical system which provides the spark to ignite the air/fuel mixture in the engine. Normally it comprises the battery, ignition coil, *distributor, (contact breaker* and *condenser),* ignition switch, *spark plugs* and wiring.
Ignition timing: See *Advance and retard.*
Inertia reel: Automatic type of safety belt which permits the wearer to move freely in normal use but which locks to give restraint on sensing either sudden deceleration of the car or sudden movement of the wearer.
In-line engine: Engine in which the *cylinders* are positioned in one row as distinct from being e.g. a *flat* or *vee* formation.

J

Jet: A calibrated nozzle or orifice in a *carburettor* through which fuel is drawn for mixing with air.
Jump leads: Heavy electric cables fitted with clips to enable a vehicle's battery to be connected to an external one for emergency starting.

K

Kerb weight: The weight of a car, unladen but ready to be driven, i.e. with enough fuel, oil etc. to travel an arbitrary distance.

Kickdown: A device used on *automatic transmissions* which allows a lower gear to be selected by flooring the accelerator.
Kingpin: A device which allows the front wheels of a car to swivel.

L

Laminated windscreen: A windscreen which has a thin plastic layer sandwiched between two layers of toughened glass. Its advantage is that it doesn't shatter or craze over when hit.
Leading shoe: Brake shoe of which the leading end (the one moved by the operating *cylinder)* is reached first by a given point on the drum during normal forward rotation. A simple single-cylinder *drum brake* will have one leading and one trailing (the opposite) shoe.
Leaf spring: A spring commonly used on cars with a *live axle,* comprising several long steel plates clamped together.
Little end: The smaller end of the *connecting rod* which is attached to the *piston.*
Live axle: An axle through which power is transmitted to the rear wheels.
Loom: A complete vehicle wiring system, or section thereof (e.g. front loom) comprising all the necessary cables of predetermined colours and lengths to wire up the various circuits.
LT: Abbreviation of low tension (meaning low voltage). Used in connection with *ignition systems.*

M

MacPherson strut: An independent front *suspension* system where the swivelling, springing and shock absorbing action of the wheel is dealt with by a single assembly.
Manifold: The device used for ducting the air/fuel mixture to the engine (inlet manifold), or the exhaust gases from the engine (exhaust manifold).
Master cylinder: A cylinder containing a *piston* and hydraulic fluid, directly coupled to a foot pedal (e.g. brake or clutch *master cylinder).* It's used for transmitting pressure to the brake or *clutch* operating mechanism.
Metallic paint: Paint finish incorporating minute particles of metal to give added lustre to the colour.
Multigrade: Lubricating oil whose *viscosity* covers that of several *monograde* oils, making it suitable for use over a wider range of operating conditions.

N

Needle bearing: Type of *bearing* in which needle or cone-shaped rollers are employed around the inner circumference, often used to reduce the space needed for the bearing.
Needle valve: A component of the *carburettor* which restricts the flow of fuel or fuel/air mixture according to its position relative to an orifice or *jet.*
Negative earth: Electrical system (now almost universally adopted) in which the negative terminal of the car battery is connected to the vehicle body, the polarity of all other electrical equipment being determined by this.

O

Octane rating: A scale rating introduced by the British Standards Institution for grading petrol.
OHC (overhead cam): Describes an engine in which the *camshaft* is situated above the *cylinder head,* and operates the *valve* gear directly without the need for *pushrods.*
OHV (overhead valve): Describes an engine which has its *valves* in the *cylinder head* (as in *OHC)* but suggests that the valve gear is operated via *pushrods* from a *camshaft* situated lower in the engine. Practically all modern car engines are OHV but are not necessarily OHC.
Oil cooler: Small *radiator* fitted in the lubricating oil circuit and sited in a cooling airflow to dissipate heat from the oil. Used mainly in higher-performance engines.
Overdrive: A device coupled to a car *gearbox* which raises the output gear ratio above the normal 1 : 1 of top gear. Also used to describe a top gear ratio of greater than 1 : 1 found in some cars.
Oversteer: A tendency for a car to turn more tightly into a corner than intended.

P

PCV (Positive crankcase ventilation): A system which allows fumes and vapours which build up in the crankcase to be drawn into the engine for burning.
Pinion: A gear with a small number of teeth which meshes with one having a larger number of teeth.
Pinking: A metallic noise from the engine often caused by the *ignition timing* being too far advanced. The noise is the result of pressure waves which cause the cylinder walls to vibrate, when the ignited fuel/air

is compressed.

Piston: Cylindrical component which slides in a closely-fitting metal tube or *cylinder* and transmits pressure. The pistons in an engine, for example, compress the fuel/air mixture, transmit the combustion power to the *crankshaft,* and exhaust the burnt gases.

Piston ring: Hardened metal ring which is a spring fit in a groove running round the *piston* to ensure a close fit to the *cylinder* wall.

Positive earth: The opposite of *negative earth.*

Propeller shaft: The shaft which transmits the drive from the *gearbox* to the rear axle in front engine/rear drive.

Pushrod: A rod which is moved up and down by the rotary motion of the *camshaft* and operates the rocker arm in an OHV engine.

Q

Quarter light: A triangular window often mounted in the front door of a car.

Quartz-halogen bulb: A bulb with a quartz envelope (instead of glass) and a tungsten filament, and filled with one of the halogen group of gases (often iodine).

R

Rack and pinion: Simplest form of steering mechanism which uses a *pinion* gear to move a toothed rack.

Radial ply tyre: A type in which the tread plies are arranged laterally, at right angles to the circumferential plane.

Radiator: Cooling device, situated in an air flow and comprising a system of fine tubes and fins for rapid heat dissipation, through which engine coolant is passed.

Radius arms (rods): Locating arms sometimes used with a *live axle* to positively locate it in the fore-and-aft direction.

Recirculating ball steering: A derivation of *worm and nut* steering, where the steering shaft motion is transmitted to the steering linkage by balls running in the groove of a worm gear.

Rev-counter: See *tachometer.*

Rocker arm: A lever which rocks on a central pivot, one end is moved up and down by the *camshaft* action and the other end operates the inlet or exhaust *valve.*

Rotor arm: A rotating arm in the *distributor* which distributes the *HT* spark voltage to the correct *spark plug.*

Running on: A tendency for an engine to keep on running after the ignition has been switched off; it's often caused by a badly maintained engine, or use of an unsuitable grade of fuel.

S

SAE: Society of Automotive Engineers (of America). The SAE classification of oils is well known but, as with *DIN* standards, SAE covers a wide range of measuring output, performance, etc, of motor vehicles.

Safety rim: A special wheel rim shape which prevents a deflated tyre from rolling off the wheel.

Sealed beam: A sealed headlamp unit where the filament is an integral part and cannot be renewed separately. Although much more expensive than separate bulbs, the illumination does not deteriorate due to contamination.

Semi-elliptic spring: *A leaf spring* used for many car rear *suspension* systems.

Semi-trailing arm: A common form of independent rear *suspension* which allows the wheel carrier to be pivoted.

Servo: A device for multiplying the normal effort applied to a control. With a brake servo, this uses the suction created in the engine inlet *manifold* to act on a *diaphragm/pushrod* for additional braking effort; it's attached to the brake *hydraulic* master *cylinder.*

Shock absorber: A device for damping out the up-and-down movement of a car when the *suspension* hits a bump in the road.

Sonic-idle carburettor: A *carburettor* where the air used for the fuel/air mixture at idle speeds is mixed in a special by-pass tube which increases the pressure drop. The velocity of the mixture increases to above the speed of sound and at the same time it becomes very turbulent which improves the fuel/air atomization.

Spark plug: A device with a ceramic insulator and two electrodes on a common metal body which screws part-way into the engine *combustion chamber.* When the *HT* voltage is applied to the plug terminal, a spark jumps the air-gap at the electrodes.

Squab: Another name for a seat cushion.

Steel-braced type: Type in which an extra ply containing steel cords is incorporated to give added strength.

Steering arm (knuckle): Short arm on the rear face of the front *stub axle* to which the steering linkage connects.

Steering rack: See *Rack and pinion.*

Stroboscopic light: A light powered from the engine

ignition system which is used for checking the ignition timing when the engine is running (i.e. dynamically).
Stroke: The total travel of the *piston* in the bore.
Stub axle: A short axle which carries the wheel only.
Sub-frame: A small frame or chassis which carries the *suspension,* and which in turn is connected to the car body.
Sump: The main oil container at the lowest part of an engine.
Suppressor: A device which is used to suppress or damp-out electrical interference caused by the *ignition system* or *generator,* wiper motor etc.
Suspension: A general term used to describe the links, springs and *dampers* with which the car body is suspended on the wheels.
Swing axle: A *suspension* arm which is pivoted near the centre-line of the car, and which gives the wheel a vertical swinging action about that pivot point.
Synchromesh: A device in a *gearbox* which synchronizes the speed of one gear shaft with another to produce smooth, noiseless engagement of the relative gears.

T

Tachometer: Also known as a rev counter, this indicates the engine speed in revolutions per minute (rpm).
Tappet: A term nowadays widely misused to refer to the adjustable parts of the valvegear of an engine. True tappets are found only in the valvegear of older engines.
Thermostat: A device which is sensitive to changes in engine temperature, and opens up an additional path for coolant to flow when the engine has warmed up.
Tie-rod (track rod): A general term for a rod which provides location for a component, or between two components (as with steering linkage).
Timing chain: Metal flexible-link chain engaging on sprocket wheels and driving the *camshaft* from the *crankshaft* in an *OHV* engine.
Timing marks: Marks normally found on the *crankshaft* pulley or *flywheel* and used for setting the ignition firing point with respect to a particular *piston.*
Toe-in/toe-out: The amount by which the front wheels point inwards or outwards, expressed either as an angle or linear measurement.
Top dead centre (tdc): The point at which a piston is at the top of its stroke.
Torque: The turning effort generated by any rotating part.

Torque converter: A coupling where the driving *torque* is transmitted through oil. At low speeds there is very little transference of torque from the input to the output; as the input shaft speed increases, the direction of fluid flow within a system of vanes alters and torque from the input impeller is transferred to the output turbine. The higher the input speed, the closer the output speed approaches it, until they are virtually the same.
Torsion bar: A spring-steel bar which turns about its own axis, and is used in some independent front *suspension* systems.
Toughened windscreen: A windscreen which will shatter in a particular way to produce blunt-edged fragments or will craze over but remain intact. A zone-toughened windscreen has a zone in front of the driver which crazes into larger parts to reduce the loss of visibility which occurs with toughened windscreens, but is otherwise similar.
Track rod: A rod which connects the steering arms to the steering gear and/or steering idler gear.
Trailing arm: A form of independent *suspension* where the wheel is attached to a swinging arm, and is mounted to the rear of the arm pivot.
Transaxle: A form of combined *gearbox* and axle from which two shafts transmit the drive to the wheels.
Transmission: A general term for a *gearbox,* but very often used as an alternative for a *transaxle.*
Two-stroke (cycle): A common term used to describe the operation of an engine where each downward piston stroke is a power stroke. The fuel/air mixture is ported into the crankcase where it's compressed by the descending *piston* and 'pumped' through another port into the *combustion chamber.* As the piston rises, the mixture is compressed and ignited, which forces the piston down. The burnt gases flow from the exhaust port, but the piston is now compressing a further charge in the crankcase which repeats the cycle. The engine needs careful design to prevent the unburnt and burnt gases from mixing and, although not a feature of the simplest designs, in some versions a rotary or reed *valve* is incorporated to help achieve this.

U

Understeer: A tendency for a car to go straight on when turned into a corner.
Universal joint: A joint that can swivel in any direction whilst at the same time transmitting *torque.* It's commonly used in *propeller shafts* and *driveshafts,* but is not suitable for some applications because the input and output shaft speeds are not the

same at all positions of angular rotation. The type in common use is known as a *Hardy-Spicer,* Hooke's or Cardan joint.

Unsprung weight: That part of a car which is not supported by the springs.

Upper cylinder lubricant (UCL): A type of light oil intended to be added to a car's fuel with the object of providing extra lubrication for the *cylinder* walls.

V

Vacuum advance: System of ignition *advance* and *retard* used in certain *distributors* where the vacuum in the engine intake *manifold* is transmitted to the distributor and acts on a *diaphragm* to alter the ignition timing according to throttle position.

Vacuum gauge: A device which indicates the amount of vacuum or suction in the inlet *manifold.*

Valve: A device which opens or closes to permit or stop gas flow into the engine.

Vee engine: Design in which the *cylinders* of an engine are set in two banks forming a V when viewed from one end. A V8, for example, consists of two such rows of four cylinders each.

Venturi: A streamlined restriction in the *carburettor* throttle bore which causes a low pressure to occur; this sucks fuel into the air stream to form a vapour suitable for combustion.

Viscosity: A term used to describe the resistance of a fluid to flow. When associated with lubricating oil it's given an *SAE* number, 10 being a very light oil and 140 being a very heavy oil.

Voltage regulator: A device which regulates the *generator* output to a predetermined level. For most *alternator* systems this is an integral part of the alternator itself, and therefore mainly applicable to *dynamo* systems. Regulators on later cars also have a device to regulate the charging current as well as the voltage.

W

Wankel engine: A rotary engine originally developed by Felix Wankel which has a triangular shaped rotor in an epitrochoidal housing (approximates in shape to a broad-waisted figure of eight). The engine has never proved popular in production cars in the UK.

Wheel balancing: Adding weights at the rim of a car wheel so that there are no out-of-balance forces.

Wishbone: An A-shaped *suspension* link, pivoted at the base of the A, and carrying a wheel at the apex. Normally mounted in an approximately horizontal plane.

Worm and nut steering: A steering system where the lower end of the steering column has a coarse screw thread on which a nut runs. The nut is attached to a spindle which carries the drop arm which, in turn, moves the steering linkage.

CONVERSION

Distance

Inches (in)	X	25.400	=	Millimetres (mm)
Feet (ft)	X	0.305	=	Metres (m)
Miles	X	1.609	=	Kilometres (km)
Millimetres (mm)	X	0.039	=	Inches (in)
Metres (m)	X	3.281	=	Feet (ft)
Kilometres (km)	X	0.621	=	Miles

Capacity

Inches, cubic (cu in/in^3)	X	16.387	=	Centimetres, cubic (cc/cm^3)
Fluid ounce, imperial (fl oz)	X	35.51	=	Centimetres, cubic (cc/cm^3)
Fluid ounce, US (fl oz)	X	29.57	=	Centimetres, cubic (cc/cm^3)
Pints, imperial (imp pt)	X	0.568	=	Litres (L)
Quarts, imperial (imp qt)	X	1.1365	=	Litres (L)
Quarts, imperial (imp qt)	X	1.201	=	Quart, US (US qt)
Quarts, US (US qt)	X	0.9463	=	Litres (L)
Quarts, US (US qt)	X	0.8326	=	Quarts, imperial (imp qt)
Gallons, imperial (imp gal)	X	4.546	=	Litres (L)
Gallons, imperial (imp gal)	X	1.201	=	Gallons, US (US gal)
Gallons, US (US gal)	X	3.7853	=	Litres (L)
Gallons, US (US gal)	X	0.8326	=	Gallons, imperial (imp gal)
Centimetres, cubic (cc/cm^3)	X	0.061	=	Inches, cubic (cu in/in^3)
Centimetres, cubic (cc/cm^3)	X	0.02816	=	Fluid ounces, imperial (fl oz)
Centimeters, cubic (cc/cm^3)	X	0.03381	=	Fluid ounces, US (fl oz)
Litres (L)	X	28.16	=	Fluid ounces, imperial (fl oz)
Litres (L)	X	33.81	=	Fluid ounces, US (fl oz)
Litres (L)	X	1.760	=	Pints, imperial (imp pt)
Litres (L)	X	0.8799	=	Quarts, imperial (imp qt)
Litres (L)	X	1.0567	=	Quarts, US (US qt)
Litres (L)	X	0.220	=	Gallons, imperial (imp gal)
Litres (L)	X	0.264	=	Gallons, US (US gal)

Area

Inches, square (in^2/sq in)	X	645.160	=	Millimetres, square (mm^2/ sq mm)
Feet,square (ft^2/sq ft)	X	0.093	=	Metres, square (m^2/sq m)
Millimetres, square (mm^2/ sq mm)	X	0.002	=	Inches, square (in^2/sq in)
Metres, square (m^2/sq m)	X	10.764	=	Feet square (ft^2/sq ft)

Weight

Ounces (oz)	X	28.350	=	Grammes (g)
Pounds (lbs)	X	0.454	=	Kilogrammes (kg)
Grammes (g)	X	0.035	=	Ounces (oz)
Kilogrammes (kg)	X	2.205	=	Pounds (lbs)
Kilogrammes (kg)	X	35.274	=	Ounces (oz)

FACTORS

Pressure

Pounds/sq in (psi/lb/sq in/ lb/in^2)	X 0.070	=	Kilogrammes/sq cm (kg/sq cm)
Pounds/sq in (psi/lb/sq in/ lb/in^2)	X 0.068	=	Atmospheres (atm)
Kilogrammes sq cm (kg/sq cm)	X 14.223	=	Pounds/sq in (psi/lb/sq in/ lb/in^2)
Atmospheres (atm)	X 14.696	=	Pounds/sq in (psi/lb/sq in/ lb/in^2)

Torque

Pound - inches (lbf in)	X 0.0115	=	Kilogramme - metres (kgf m)
Pound - inches (lbf in)	X 0.0833	=	Pound - feet (lbf ft)
Pound - feet (lbf ft)	X 12	=	Pound - inches (lbf in)
Pound - feet (lbf ft)	X 0.138	=	Kilogramme - metres (kgf m)
Pound - feet (lbf ft)	X 1.356	=	Newton - metres (Nm)
Kilogramme - metres (kgf m)	X 86.796	=	Pound - inches (lbf in)
Kilogramme - metres (kgf m)	X 7.233	=	Pound - feet (lbf ft)
Newton - metres (Nm)	X 0.738	=	Pound - feet (lbf ft)
Newton - metres (Nm)	X 0.102	=	Kilogramme - metres (kgf m)

Speed

Miles - hour (mph)	X 1.609	=	Kilometres - hour (kph)
Feet - second	X 0.305	=	Metres - second (m/s)
Kilometres - hour (kph)	X 0.621	=	Miles - hour (mph)
Metres - second (m/s)	X 3.281	=	Feet - second
Metres - second (m/s)	X 3.600	=	Kilometres - hour (kph)

Consumption

Miles - gallon, imperial (mpg)	X 0.354	=	Kilometres - litre (km/l)
Kilometres - litre (km/l)	X 2.825	=	Miles - gallon, imperial (mpg)

Temperature

Centigrade (°C) to Fahrenheit (°F)

$$\frac{9}{5}\,^{o}C + 32 = {}^{o}F$$

Fahrenheit (°F) to Centigrade (°C)

$$\frac{5}{9}\,({}^{o}F - 32) = {}^{o}C$$

Index

Printed by
J H Haynes & Co Ltd
Sparkford Nr Yeovil
Somerset BA22 7JJ England